Jesus and Courageous Women

Elsa Tamez

[signature]

Study Guide by

Sallie M. Cuffee

Jesus and Courageous Women
copyright © 2001 Elsa Tamez

Study Guide for *Jesus and Courageous Women*
copyright © 2001 Women's Division

A publication of the Women's Division
produced by the General Board of Global Ministries
The United Methodist Church
475 Riverside Drive
New York, New York 10115

Printed in the United States of America
Library of Congress Catalog Card Number: 00-135480

Cover design: John Havey

Please address critiques or comments to the Editor of Program Resources
Room 1478
General Board of Global Ministries, The United Methodist Church
475 Riverside Drive
New York, New York 10115.

Contents

Word from the Author

I have decided to use the traditional Jewish method of biblical interpretation called midrash* to tell the stories of the courageous women who followed Jesus. Through the first person Lydia ("I, Lydia"), we hear these valuable testimonies of early women that motivate us, as women of the church today, to rethink our lives in relation to the church and to society. Many other testimonies of women of faith who love, struggle, resist, and teach could be added to these selected biblical testimonies.

Through Lydia's voice and perspective in the early church (see Acts 16: 11-15, 40), I present some courageous women of the movement of Jesus, the Christ. I have opted to speak of the "movement of Jesus" and not about Jesus as an isolated person for two reasons. First of all, to speak of Jesus as an isolated individual does not reflect historical reality. The Jesus we know from the Gospels was always accompanied by his disciples and followers (the majority peasants, including fishermen and tradespeople) who placed their hopes in Jesus' preaching and teaching about the Kingdom of God. This was a movement of renewal that was to occur first in local communities and then to spread among the people of Palestine; Jesus of Nazareth was its founding leader.[1] The second reason for using this approach is that it allows us to draw near to Jesus today, not just as the person who loves us as individuals, but as the one who offers us a community project of new life, and challenges us to engage in both personal and social transformation.

I am aware that there are differences between the movement of Jesus of Nazareth in Palestine and the Christian movement beyond Palestine. The commonly noted ones arise from the fact that the movement of Jesus refers to an internal renewal of Judaism before "Christianity" began as a distinct faith. The propagation of

* Words marked this way are defined in the Glossary on page 171.

the Gospel after Jesus' resurrection, especially as it occurred beyond Palestine, corresponds to a missionary movement. It led to the establishment of Christian communities especially among Gentiles although it did not exclude the Jews. I prefer to speak of only one movement, however, as it represents a counter-movement to the dominance of the Roman Empire. I believe that for women particularly it is vital to emphasize the continuity of the movement of Jesus beyond Palestine. It is there that we find the greater expression of the movement's liberating force in its confrontation with the patriarchal oppression of the Roman Empire and practices of Judaism. This force continues to be present in the early Christian communities toward the middle of the first century. To signify this continuity, I have added the words "the Christ" to the term "the movement of Jesus."

The sometimes sharp criticism that Jesus thrusts at his own Jewish culture does not reflect an anti-Jewish stance. As we know, Jesus is a Jew and therefore places himself in a position of self-critique with respect to the patriarchy of Judaism and Roman culture as enacted in oppressive practices. Importantly, in this same way, women today engage in constructive criticism of their religious and social cultures.

I have organized the women's stories beginning with those who gathered at the cross because these women demonstrate most dramatically the tremendous risks that being near to the cross meant in the context of Roman society and the great courage it took to be there. The choice of the passage from the Gospel of John simply responds to the fact that women described in this passage clearly represent my objectives. Certainly we see courage, love, faithfulness, struggle, resistance, and discipleship in the four women at the cross. However, I also see in them three different types of women as the narrator Lydia explains in the Introduction.

I have chosen the biblical character Lydia as the fictitious narrator of these stories as a way of introducing the reader to the ancient world. As a literary device, she allows me to emphasize the continuity of the movement of Jesus outside Palestine, and at the same time to offer, in a more familiar way, the cultural elements of the time. Perhaps Lydia was not aware of all the women's stories, but surely she had heard many of them. Lydia also helps us to see that Paul, who does not explicitly mention the life of Jesus, was neither the first nor the only one involved in the spreading of the movement.

Anachronisms* are inevitable in Lydia. Lydia was a leader of the Christian movement in Philippi approximately 20 years after the death of Jesus. Obviously anachronisms are reflected in my modern viewpoint and most probably as well from the decades after the life of Lydia. As we know, the Gospels were written well after Jesus' time. The issues and problems they raise differ according to the objectives of each evangelist and the situation of the readers.[2] This fact, however, does not alter my intention to propose a re-reading of these passages that we may discover, in the movement of Jesus, the Christ, the criteria which will illuminate the practices of the church today with regard to the role and inclusion of women.

Notes

1. Richard A. Horsley, *Sociology and the Movement of Jesus* (New York: Continuum, 1994), pp. 116-118.

2. We do not enter into a discussion of whether the events related in the passages existed in reality or are creations of the authors of the Gospels.

Introduction

Lydia, the Narrator

I, Lydia, will tell these stories. I'm from Thyatira (in Asia Minor) and live in Philippi. I belong to the movement of Jesus, the Christ. I didn't know Jesus, the founder of this movement, personally. But from the moment I heard about him and his movement in Galilee through Paul and Silas (Acts 16: 11-55), I decided to become a part of the Christian communities that were growing outside of Palestine. These communities carried with them the spirit of the movement of Jesus, the man from Galilee.[1] I am a Gentile, converted to Judaism and now to Christianity.[2] My life has changed radically since I began to participate in the Christian communities, which for me are an extension of the movement of Jesus. As a woman, I can state that the movement of Jesus within and outside of Palestine has made it possible for women to be considered persons of worth, capable of participating on an equal footing with men in the communities. Of course there are discussions and difficulties within the communities themselves, but we cannot deny the fact that there have been great steps forward with respect to the participation of women. In fact, it is our significant presence as women that generates these discussions.[3]

When stories are written down, women are usually not taken into account, in spite of the fact that we are frequently the storytellers! Our patriarchal* societies consider it natural for men to create and record history.[4] Historical reality, however, is very different. Women do participate actively. Many stories have reached my ears about women in the movement of Jesus in Galilee and Judea and later in places outside of Palestine. It disturbs me that when the stories of Jesus are told in our gatherings, he seems to be accompanied

---

* Words marked with an asterisk are defined in the Glossary on page 171.

only by men, the twelve. This is not the way it was! I realize that twelve is a symbolic number that represents the 12 tribes led by the Messiah Jesus. But women accompanied him all the time as well (Lk. 8: 1-3). They even followed him from Galilee to Jerusalem, and were with him the week he was sentenced to death.[5]

The stories I've heard about the women followers of Jesus tell me two important things: first, that Jesus has a special inclination for those people at the marginalized* sectors of society, such as women, the poor and the sick, and all those who are discriminated against; and second, that we women have found in the movement of Jesus the hope and vision that things can be different for us, because until Jesus' time, we had always been shoved aside. So I am eager to tell you what I know about the movement of Jesus, the one we call the Christ, and of the courageous women who followed him. Let me begin by telling you about the setting in which the movement arose.

The Movement of Jesus and Its Context

The situation in Palestine during the time of Jesus was difficult and full of conflict. After the death of Jesus, things got even worse. Palestine was then, and is now, a land occupied by a foreign power, the Roman Empire; Roman troops move about the area constantly. To see foreign troops occupying your territory is not at all pleasant. I am very familiar with the Roman soldiers; many live here in Philippi, since it is a Roman colony. Many aspects of life in this colony are overshadowed by military presence.[6] Besides that, the many different taxes we must pay to the Roman Empire are a great burden. Add to these the Temple tax that the Jews, even in the Diaspora,* had to send to Jerusalem.[7] Jesus did not look favorably upon this tax.

The birthplace of the movement of Jesus was Galilee, a largely rural region, in spite of the presence of several Greek cities in the area. The majority of the population of the province is dedicated to agriculture (some say between 80 and 90%),[8] especially the cultivation of olives, figs, and vineyards. Jesus loved to use examples from the fields to talk about the Good News, which he called the Kingdom of God (Mt. 13: 24-30; Mk. 4: 26-32). He had moved throughout the countryside his entire life. He was from Nazareth, an insignificant little town with few inhabitants, located on a cliff and surrounded by cliffs. The views in Galilee are beautiful. I don't think Jesus liked the cities. Hellenistic* Greek cities appear similar; their architecture is impressive. I've never been in Sepphoris, the most important city of Galilee, about three miles from Nazareth,[9] but I imagine that it is very much like Philippi where I live. It probably has a theater, gymnasium, baths, and the beautiful homes of the rich. Greek is spoken in these cities, as it is here in Philippi. Although Jews also live here, Aramaic, the language of Jesus, is not spoken.

I say that Jesus didn't like the cities because I have never heard any story that mentions Sepphoris, and surely Jesus was there many times. He may have worked there as a carpenter or in construction work with his father, because three miles is not far for a peasant to walk.[10] He couldn't have survived as a carpenter by working only in Nazareth with its mere 500 inhabitants. However, Jesus did spend time in Bethsaida and Chorazin. But he didn't have many good things to say about these places and even pronounced some "woes" over them (Mt. 11: 21; Lk. 10: 13). When Jesus began his ministry, he went to Capernaum. Some think he went there to work in the city of Tiberias that Herod Antipas began to build after overseeing the rebuilding of Sepphoris. Capernaum was not really a city, but a large town of some 1,000 people;[11] of course it was a much more important place than Nazareth. From Capernaum Jesus traveled to towns and cities to speak of the Kingdom of God.

Capernaum is on the edge of the Sea of Galilee, where the fishing industry is a source of riches, though the independent fishermen certainly do not reap the benefits. The moneychangers and governors become rich![12] Many of the stories I have heard about Jesus—the healings, the miracles and the casting out of demons—happened in the different towns and cities that are on the edges of the Sea of Galilee, or Tiberias, as it is also called. I can't forget to mention that one of the best known and loved disciples of Jesus was Mary Magdalene, from Magdala, another town that borders the lake.

As I was saying, at this time the political situation was already very difficult. In the year 4, when Jesus was still a child, Sepphoris had been plundered by the Romans because the citizens of that city, Hellenized Jews, rebelled against the Roman Empire and lost. It must have been a humiliating experience, and it undoubtedly left a mark on Jesus as a child, and on his family. This is only one example. I have heard of many more conflicts between the Romans and the people, especially in Galilee,[13] a region where conflict prevailed. Many indebted peasants lost their land and then had no choice but to go to prison for their debts—or to join anti-Roman movements and hide out in caves. There were then and exist today several movements that seek to muster the people's aspirations. There are prophetic movements, messianic movements and others that operate more like groups of bandits. The poor sympathize with these groups because they rob the rich to give to the poor.[14] Some believe that the two bandits crucified with Jesus came from these groups. Ordinary thieves are never crucified, only slaves and subversives. The Roman troops are very powerful and have crushed many movements, leaving many people dead.

When I think about Jesus and the context in which he lived, I understand why so many people followed him. Jesus' every gesture, word, and deed responded to his followers' dreams of hope. Because they sought newness of life in Jesus, they joined his movement. I also understand why his life was in danger so many times, and why the Pharisees and Scribes and the High Priest wanted to take him prisoner. They were afraid that his movement would be seen as anti-Roman, and that the troops of the Empire would wipe out this province that was already considered rebellious. Jesus consecrated his whole life to showing us a different way to live from the way we live now in this Roman society. That's why I have come to love him so much, and admire his life, and consider myself to be a disciple of the risen Christ. Jesus believed there must be room for all in society—women and men, the poor, the sick, and the ignorant. The Kingdom of God, the central proclamation of Jesus, is an ideal Realm in which there is no war, no domination of one people over another, no hunger, no discrimination, for all people are viewed as precious, loved, and valued in God's eyes.

Women and the Movement of Jesus

There were women in the movement of Jesus, and not merely a few. Women, too, were disciples, and they followed him just as the men did (Lk. 8: 1-3).[15] Jesus did not make a distinction between women and men. On the contrary, one of the characteristics of his teaching was to propose an order different from the hierarchical* order we know. He was daring in his teachings; he did not side with those who wanted to occupy the highest positions. He spoke out against the political authorities who dominated the rest of the people. "Among you it will not be so" (Mt. 10: 42-45), he said. And he did not speak well of the religious authorities who believed themselves to be very righteous, who marginalized those they considered "impure," and took advantage of widows.

For me, Lydia, this message that includes me, that considers me to be a daughter of God, free and important, is what has given meaning to my life and my community. I believe that many women feel the same way. I also like Jesus' self-critical view. As a Jewish man, he saw the ways that Jewish society discriminates against women. Many times women are considered to be impure and are not allowed to take on important roles in the synagogues. Perhaps because Jesus was from Galilee and not Judea, he didn't give much importance to the traditions within Jewish law and culture that push women to the side.[16] Jesus allowed himself to be surrounded and followed by women. He considered them to be equal to men. He re-established their dignity and worth that had been eradicated by the customs of a patriarchal society.

In the movement of Jesus there were more women than we've been led to believe. This is, in part, because so much emphasis has been placed on the twelve male disciples.[17] But again, this is a symbolic number. In reality there were many women who listened to his teachings and followed him as disciples wherever he went. Nobody can deny that when he went to Jerusalem the week of his death, several women accompanied him from Galilee. All the accounts I've heard about the resurrection of Jesus mention several women witnesses (Mk. 16: 5-7, 9-11; Mt. 28: 1-8; Lk. 24: 1-10; Jn. 20). Mary Magdalene is in all of those accounts. I firmly believe that women were present at community meals with Jesus,[18] and that like the men they were also sent to teach and heal. This is what I do now in Philippi. I am active in the community and teach like any man. There are many influential women, but we are not often mentioned in the Gospel accounts. Just because Peter, James, and John are spoken of often, as well as Andrew, does that mean that only men belonged to the movement?

When I listen to stories about Jesus, more men appear as his followers. Although women often appear as those who are healed or helped, many women also sought Jesus because they saw in him and in his movement the prospect for a new quality of life. And Jesus always listened to their petitions. Frequently, these women were poor and very needy; but many men in this same situation also sought Jesus. I've also heard of women of a more elevated social status, such as Joanna and Susanna (Joanna was the wife of Chuza, the administrator for Herod Agrippa, Governor of Galilee), who not only followed Jesus but provided economic support for his movement. I am not rich, but neither am I poor, for I sell the purple cloth that I import from Thyatira and live like any other artisan or merchant; sometimes things go well, sometimes not so well.[19]

Something that attracts me and other women to Jesus is his understanding of family. For him family are those who listen and do the will of God; that is, men and women, parents and children— all are brothers and sisters (Mt. 12: 46-50; Mk. 3: 31-35; Lk. 8: 19-21). This is not to say that he was against the *traditional* family. Rather he was opposed to the *patriarchal* concept of family. Here in Roman culture, as well as in Jewish culture, women have been given a very defined role of submission. The ideal life for a woman is to be a mother, stay at home, and obey her husband because he is the head of the household. The Roman society here in Philippi and in other Roman provinces is very critical of women who do not follow this prescribed role. Because those of us in the Christian communities seek a life free of discrimination, following our founder Paul who says "there is no longer Jew or Greek, there is no longer slave or free, there is no longer male and female" (Gal. 3: 28), we become the target of criticism.

In some Christian communities, such as Corinth and others (see 1 Cor. 11: 2-16), we know that discussions and conflict concerning our participation are taking place, and we are losing some of the progress that has been made. I imagine that the same thing happened in the movement of Jesus in Galilee, although not to the same extent as what we see here. I hope and pray we will not lose sight of his basic teachings. If our participation as women continues to be restricted as some are saying, even if the reason is to allow for the survival of the Christian communities, I fear we will stray from the fundamental elements of the Kingdom of God as pronounced by Jesus.

One of the problems may be that the women of Galilee who followed Jesus to Jerusalem (Mk. 15: 40-41) probably returned to

Galilee after his death. Several renowned disciples, however, remained in Jerusalem. The women quite possibly founded communities, but little by little they disappeared from the story. I ask myself, what happened to Martha and Mary, the two women who were such good friends of Jesus? They were from Bethany, a place close to Jerusalem. Martha had made an eloquent confession of faith that Jesus was the Messiah (Jn. 11: 27). And this is why I and many other women of the Christian movement have a great responsibility. We must tell the stories again from our point of view, taking into account the fact that there are many of us who are now community leaders. In this way we can express resistance to the patriarchal culture that little by little restricts our full participation in our own society.

Women Near the Cross

They say that the day Jesus was taken prisoner on the Mount of Olives, the disciples were very afraid, and rightfully so. Those crucified who were not slaves were seen as subversives, enemies of the Roman Empire. It was clear that Jesus was considered a subversive. It was even worse when the soldiers put a sign on him, mockingly or not, calling him "Jesus, the King of the Jews" (Mt. 27:37). To call oneself the son of God was a provocation; for the Romans only the Emperor was the son of God. It was very dangerous, therefore, to be identified with Jesus the Galilean.[20] They almost found Peter out because of his Galilean accent and he was forced to deny that he was one of Jesus' followers (Mk. 14: 66-72). I heard that all of them hid together in a house for fear of being imprisoned and condemned (see Jn. 20: 19). However, it is also said that many women who followed Jesus stood watching from far off (Mk.15: 40; Mt. 27: 55-56; Lk. 23: 49). One account describes how some women gathered near the cross (Jn. 19: 25). I don't understand how this could have been. Generally the area of a crucifixion is full of soldiers and no one, not even family members or friends, is allowed near. They are not permitted to cry or to mourn.[21] In any case I do believe, as all the stories mention, that the women were there at a distance, accompanying their Master, the leader of the movement, in those moments of great agony. Those Galilean women had to have been very brave not to lock themselves up in their homes as did many other men and women disciples (Jn. 20: 19).

How I would've liked to have known more about the women who were near the cross! But the stories I've heard are somewhat confusing and mention various names. One account says that "Mary Magdalene, Mary the mother of James and Joses, and Salome" (Mk. 15: 40f) were at the cross. Another says that it was Mary Magdalene, Mary the mother of James and Joses, and the mother of the sons of Zebedee (Mt. 27: 55). Another simply refers to the women from Galilee who had followed and served Jesus (Lk. 23: 49). And when it mentions the tomb, it says that among them were Mary Magdalene, Joanna, Mary the mother of James, and others who were with them (Lk. 24:10). Although there is some confusion about the names, Mary Magdalene's is always present and listed first. This indicates that her presence was undeniable and memorable and that she was accompanied by other women.

These women who did not hide (Jn. 20:19) would have also been afraid. However, they were willing to risk observing from afar everything that happened. They especially noticed the location of the tomb where the body had been laid; perhaps they intended to embalm him. But what is most significant is that all the stories say that the resurrected Jesus appeared first to the women and charged them with telling the other disciples (Mk. 16: 5-7; Mt. 28: 5-7; Lk. 24: 5-10). This clearly indicates that Jesus inaugurated a movement in which women participated equally with men. We have to recognize that this was difficult for some of the disciples to understand. The weight of their patriarchal heritage and context is heavy and even though Jesus taught and practiced equality in relationships among men and women, many of the male disciples did not follow his example. Even Paul, who is often accompanied by women in his ministry and has in fact been imprisoned along with women due to persecution (Rom. 16: 7), fails to mention that the resurrected Jesus appeared first to the women (1 Cor. 15: 3-8). The cultural burden is heavy, which is why I, Lydia, insist that we need to return to the principles of equality of the movement of Jesus.

Another story tells that there were four women and a man, John (Jn. 19: 25-27), near the cross. This story is unique and I have not heard it elsewhere. I want to use this story to illustrate women who are symbols of courage, precisely because they were near Jesus during his crucifixion. The story says that four women were present: Mary the mother of Jesus; Mary's sister who is Jesus' aunt; Mary, the wife of Clopas; and Mary Magdalene (Jn. 19: 25). Mary, Jesus' mother, is a woman who gives herself in love, for she loved her son and certainly, as a woman, was marked by the life and death of her son. Women like her are those who love and dare, and I will tell you more about them in the first chapter.

We know nothing about Jesus' aunt or the wife of Clopas. They represent those women who are marginalized, but who, in spite of their marginalization and invisibility, struggle and resist. Mary Magdalene is an exemplary disciple, a leader of the movement. She represents the women disciples and teachers who are abundant today especially outside of Palestine in Corinth, Philippi, Ephesus, Rome, and other cities. All of these women are disciples: loving, stubborn and daring. I describe them this way to help organize their stories.

Notes

1. Although there are differences between the movement of Jesus in Galilee and the missionary movement launched after the resurrection (cf. Elisabeth Schüssler Fiorenza, *In Memory of Her, A Feminist Theological Reconstruction of Christian Origins* [New York: The Crossroad Publishing Co., 1994], pp. 99-104, I agree with Luise Schottroff in identifying only one liberation movement in the face of the Pax Romana. See *Lydia's Impatient Sisters: A Feminist Social History of Early Christianity* (Louisville: Westminster John Knox Press, 1995), p. 9.

2. At that time Christians were considered a branch of Judaism. The people continued to participate in both the synagogue and in house-churches.

3. See pages 97-102 of this book: "Let Women Not Be Silent in the Congregation."

4. Elisabeth Schüssler Fiorenza states: "Women have always transmitted history, told stories and kept memories alive. However, history has by and large been written by elite men as their own story and in their own interests." *But She Said: Feminist Practices of Biblical Interpretation* (Boston: Beacon Press, 1992), p. 80.

5. Carla Ricci suggests a hypothesis concerning an "exegesis of silence." In view of the scarcity of sources, we must study the biblical texts differently in these

cases where women are barely taken into account or forgotten altogether. Ricci suggests that we must question the silences, not the words. The silence and deliberate absence of the presence of women in the texts reveal a culture that excluded women. *Mary Magdalene and Many Others: Women Who Followed Jesus* (Minneapolis: Fortress Press, 1994), pp. 19ff.

6. José Comblin, *Epístola aos Filipenses* (Petrópolis: Vozes, 1985), p. 7.

7. The Jews of the Diaspora also paid the Temple tax. After the destruction of Jerusalem in 70 C.E., the tax was passed on to the treasury of the Roman Empire, designated for the temple of Jupiter.

8. K.C. Hanson and Douglas E. Oakman, *Palestine in the Time of Jesus: Social Structures and Social Conflicts* (Minneapolis: Fortress Press, 1988), p. 104.

9. A little more than three miles.

10. The silence in the Gospels about this city is remarkable due to the short distance between Nazareth and Sepphoris. Jesus' family must have taken notice of all the events that occurred in that beautiful city, capital of the province of Galilee.

11. Richard A. Horsley, *Galilee: History, Politics, People* (Valley Forge, Penn.: Trinity Press International, 1995), p. 195.

12. Hanson and Oakman list the beneficiaries, beginning with the emperors who benefited from the port taxes, including all types of tax collectors and ending with the merchants who salt the fish. *Palestine in the Time of Jesus*, pp. 108-109.

13. See John Dominic Crossan, *The Historical Jesus: The Life of a Mediterranean Jewish Peasant* (San Francisco: HarperCollins, 1991), pp. 124-136; Richard Horsley, *Jesus and the Spiral of Violence: Popular Jewish Resistance in Roman Palestine* (San Francisco: Harper & Row, 1987); Gerard Theissen, *A la sombra del Galileo. Las investigaciones históricas sobre Jesús traducidas a un relato* (Salamanca: Sígueme, 1988). The problem with this last book is that it reduces the conflict to the Zealot movement, which probably gained strength at the beginning of the 60s C.E.

14. R. Horsley and John S. Hanson, *Bandits, Prophets and Messiahs: Popular*

Movements in the Time of Jesus (New Voices in Biblical Studies, eds. Adela Yarbro Collins and John J. Collins [Minneapolis: Winston Press, Seabury Books], 1985; J. Crossan, *The Historical Jesus*, pp. 209-250.

15. Carla Ricci presents an excellent analysis of Luke 8: 1-3. She considers this to be a text forgotten by those who do exegesis. When the text is not taken into account, an exegetical distortion occurs with respect to the presence of women in the movement of Jesus. *Mary Magdalene and Many Others*, pp. 29ff.

16. Horsley, *Galilee*, pp. 156, 235-237.

17. For the Gospels and Acts, the number 12 is more important than the actual names. In fact there is confusion concerning the names of the twelve, for they don't even all appear; the Gospels contradict each other in this. See Suzanne Tunc, *También las mujeres seguían a Jesús* (Santander: Sal Terrae, 1999), pp. 25-38.

18. Ibid., pp. 59-65.

19. It is most likely that she is not of a high social status as has traditionally been believed. New research shows that the purple for the cloth that she sold was not extracted from mollusks, but from a plant common in Thyatira. See Ivoni Richter Reimer, *Vida de Mulheres na Sociedade e na Igreja* (São Paulo: Paulinas, 1995), pp. 73ff. We will explore this in more detail in chapter 9 in the section on Priscilla and Lydia.

20. Concerning the risks that women faced in the context of the crucifixion, see Luise Schottroff, *Mulheres no Novo Testamento. Exegese numa Perspectiva Feminista* (São Paulo: Paulinas, 1995), pp. 44-48.

21. Ivoni Richter Reimer quotes the following fragment of the Roman historian Tacitus in the *Annals* 6: 19 about mass executions: "There was an enormous mountain of dead, of both sexes, of all ages, people of noble origin and simple. It was not permitted for family members and friends to draw near to cry over their dead, not even were they allowed to gaze on them for more time. The guards were placed on all sides and watched carefully to see if someone showed signs of mourning." "Recordar, transmitir, actuar. Mujeres en los comienzos del cristianismo" in *Revista de Interpretación Bíblica Latinoamericana* (RIBLA), no. 22 (1995), p. 50.

Chapter 1

Mary, Mother of the Leader of the Movement

(Matthew 12: 46-50; Luke 1: 26-56; 2: 1-7; 2: 41-50;
John 2: 1-12; 19: 25)

I, Lydia, have heard very little about Mary. What I have heard sometimes makes me think that Mary didn't belong to the movement of Jesus. During Jesus' ministry, she, along with her other children, only appears once in awhile seeking Jesus among the multitudes (Mt. 12: 46-50; Mk. 3: 31-32; Lk. 8: 19-21). What is clear is that after the death of her son, Mary was involved in the movement of Jesus, the Christ, and participated in the community in Jerusalem (Acts 1: 14). The community met in the upper part of a house in Jerusalem. It is said that this community of men and women met and persevered in prayer with one same Spirit (Acts 2: 42-47).

That's all that I have heard about her relationship to the movement. However, I'm sure she was very active. Generally when women are included in history, the fact that they are mentioned at all is more significant than it would first appear. So Mary, the mother of Jesus, possibly became involved in the movement either shortly before the death of her son, or shortly afterward, at his rising from the dead.[1]

It is Mary, however, who has always captured my attention. I find something special about her for having been the woman who brought into the world Jesus of Nazareth, whom we, the Christians of Philippi, know as the Messiah, the Son of God. Two things about her stand out to me: the way she is described in the biblical stories; and what it would mean to be the mother of a person like Jesus.

A Son Is Announced to Mary and She Sings with Joy

One of the stories about the announcement of the birth of Jesus (Lk. 1: 26-38) begins with an angel who appeared to her and said, "Greetings, favored one! The Lord is with you" (Lk. 1: 28). This identification of an angel of the Lord with this humble young woman (for surely she was very young, perhaps 12 or 13) is one of the characteristics of our movement: God identifies with those who are lowly or deemed unimportant in society. In this greeting we see that God gives her the respect she deserves. She is not simply an instrument to be utilized.[2]

Mary was from Nazareth in Galilee, a rural town with fewer than 500 inhabitants.[3] God didn't choose the wife of Herod the Great, for example, or one of the distinguished wives of the Temple leaders who live in the beautiful city of Jerusalem. God chose to be born in an insignificant town through the womb of a young peasant woman.

Mary, of course, was frightened, but the angel Gabriel told her not to be afraid and announced that she would be the mother of the Son of the Most High.[4] Mary was very familiar with the tradition of her Jewish people. She recognized in the words of the angel the words that she had heard before in messianic promises. Imagine her tremendous surprise and joy at this astounding news; not only did she hear the announcement of the coming of the Messiah, awaited anxiously in the context of Roman domination, but she, a poor woman, had been chosen by God to bring forth the Messiah!

Mary had not yet married Joseph, but she knew they would be married someday. According to Jewish custom, the parents arrange the children's marriage like a contract. Later they are married. Years can go by between the time of the contract and the time of the wedding.[5] Thus she asked how she could possibly give birth without a husband. The angel explained that the child would be born of the Holy Spirit (Lk. 1: 35). Mary of Nazareth accepted this news. She would face the challenge of being an unwed mother in the eyes of society, accepting the risk that her future husband might reject her for being pregnant before marriage. She would also risk being stoned to death for adultery. She accepted these enormous challenges because she believed the word of the angel, and replied: "Here am I, the servant of the Lord; let it be with me according to your word" (Lk. 1: 38). In another account, the angel appears only to Joseph. Joseph was going to abandon her for becoming pregnant by someone else. But the angel tells Joseph that the child is of the Holy Spirit, and that it will be Jesus, the Savior—and asks him not to leave Mary (Mt. 1: 18-25). I see that Mary does not participate at all in this dialogue. The fact that everything is decided between the angel and Joseph makes it seem to me to be a very patriarchal story.

I have also heard the impressive song of Mary. She sang it after visiting her cousin Elizabeth who was also pregnant.[6] There was a profound and deeply shared joy at this meeting of the two women. They were very different, for Elizabeth was a distinguished woman, a descendant of Aaron and wife of Zechariah, a priest. They lived close to the great city of Jerusalem. In contrast, Mary was a humble peasant woman of unknown lineage who lived in an insignificant village. Yet both were blessed by God: Elizabeth because God gave her a son after many years of barrenness and so gave her dignity and worth as a woman (Lk. 1: 25). Mary was blessed because God found grace in her, a humble peasant. We learn that when they met, Elizabeth's baby jumped within her, and she became aware of the role for which Mary's baby was destined. Isn't it amazing that a baby, even from within its mother's body, can communicate things of God?[7] Elizabeth praised Mary's faith because Mary believed in and trusted the angel's words. Zechariah, meantime, had a hard time believing the angel's promise that in his old age he would become a father. For his disbelief he was struck dumb. They then say that Mary, inspired by Hannah's song (1 Sam. 2: 1-10) and other verses of Scripture, began to praise God for God's mercy toward the lowly that was manifested in her. She sang: "My soul magnifies the Lord and my spirit rejoices in God my

Savior, for he has looked with favor on the lowliness of his servant." Some interpret this as "the littleness or humility of his servant," but I believe that here lowliness refers to humiliation and social marginalization, be it from barrenness, rape, or low social status.[8]

Mary said that the generations would call her blessed and I'm sure that will always be true. Even as I tell her story, so you will tell it after me. In this song Mary remembered the merciful ways of God toward the poor, lowly, and hungry. She saw in the coming Messiah the love of God for Israel, God's people, and remembered God's promises to the fathers, beginning with Abraham. The degradation of Mary is the degradation her people have suffered.[9] For example, Nazareth was very close to Sepphoris, a city that was devastated by the Romans when Jesus was just a child. The destruction of a town by a more powerful one is a humiliation. I believe that Mary noticed and felt the humiliations that her people suffered. Like Mary, I believe that inequality between human beings displeases God. This is why in the movement of Jesus before and after his death, we always remember the poor.

Of all the stories I have heard about Mary, this one impresses me the most. Through her song and the meeting with the angel, I see a very courageous woman in Mary. This courage is apparent as well when we hear that she, along with three other women and John (Jn. 19: 24),[10] were near the cross when her son Jesus was being crucified; all the other disciples and followers had fled in fear and went into hiding. As a woman, I can imagine what it must have been like to be the mother of a person like Jesus, the leader of a new movement. Certainly it took faith and courage for her to accept the lifestyle of such a son. It could not have been easy.

The Sorrow and Satisfaction That Mary Experienced

As I think about all the stories I've heard about Mary and Jesus, I cannot help but conclude that Mary, as a woman and mother, must have suffered over and cried much for her son. He must have caused her, unintentionally, many heartaches and headaches—sometimes due to difficulties involved in raising and educating children, and at other times because Jesus had plans that Mary found difficult to understand.

For example, when she was pregnant with Jesus, Mary was forced to travel from Nazareth to Bethlehem. It would have been very uncomfortable because she would have had to walk several days and many miles. And from what I hear, she was just about ready to give birth. Mary and Joseph had to travel to Bethlehem because the Roman Emperor Augustus ordered the provinces to do a census of the population. This meant that everyone, including those in the cities and/or rural areas, had to declare all their possessions for the official register in order to estimate the amount that should be taxed. Perhaps Joseph owned a plot of land in Bethlehem and needed to declare it. Wives were obliged to travel with their husbands.[11] The objective of the census was to broaden the system of taxation. Actions like this often created fear among the poor or in entire communities that were not a part of the dominant culture due to political, ethnic or racial differences or status. A peasant or artisan, such as a carpenter, could expect to pay up to half his or her income due to the many different kinds of taxes.[12]

Upon arrival in Bethlehem, Mary was forced to give birth in a stable because they were unable to find a more adequate place to stay. This would not have been so difficult a situation for a peasant woman, however. Nazareth, her home, was in a rural area. But it would not be pleasant to give birth in a town and place where she was a stranger rather than in her own home. But I don't believe any of this happened by chance. We see in it God's intention to bring the Messiah into the world precisely in a social context that was familiar to many marginalized peoples. The apostle Paul exhorted us once with these words: "Let the same mind be in you that was in Christ Jesus, who, though he was in the form of God, did not regard equality with God as something to be exploited, but emptied himself, taking the form of a slave..." (Phil. 2: 2-7).

Mothers like Mary feel very protective of their children and watch over them until they reach maturity.[13] You can imagine the suffering and anguish of a mother who knows her son is in danger of death. Mary first experienced this agony when she found out that Herod wanted to destroy her child. She must have been desperate when she fled to Egypt with Joseph and Jesus, and could only be at peace when Herod died. The stories don't tell us all the details about her feelings; but we can imagine it must have been this way because the characters of these stories are people of flesh and blood and have feelings. I have these same feelings and I observe them in other mothers.

There is a story about Mary and Joseph's visit to Jerusalem for the festival of the Passover (Lk. 2: 41-51). Jesus must have been about 13 years old, which was considered to be the year young boys enter manhood. This explains why he was traveling separately from his parents. His parents had traveled an entire day before realizing the Jesus was not in the caravan with them returning to Nazareth. (It was dangerous to travel alone so people traveled together in caravans.) The frantic parents Mary and Joseph searched everywhere they would have expected a young man of Jesus' age to be, but couldn't find him. It wasn't until the third day that they found him in the Temple giving evidence of his unusual insight and intelligence as he listened to and questioned the rabbis. Mary, responsible for protecting and educating her son according to the customs of the Mediterranean world, scolded him for his lack of consideration toward his parents who had searched frantically for him. Surely she was furious with Jesus because of the scare he had given her and because he was holding up the caravan. Or perhaps the caravan had gone on and they would now have to return alone, which was even more dangerous. At any rate, we don't know exactly what she was thinking. Jesus doesn't excuse himself and that must have hurt Mary. As his mother she would have expected his loyalty and respect, in keeping with the custom.[14] Jesus told them that they should already have been aware of the fact that he was different, and that his duty was to begin to take responsibility for the things of God, who was his father. We learn that neither Mary nor Joseph understood this answer. Fortunately for Mary, Jesus decided to return with them and remained a part of the household, like any other son, for a while longer.

Although not being able to find Jesus caused Mary anguish, it must also have filled her with pride to find him among the teachers as if he were one of them. To see a son develop and mature is a satisfaction that mothers never forget. That is why she carried all these experiences in her heart, even though she couldn't understand them. It seems that this was foretelling the break Jesus would have with his birth family, not because he wanted it, but because he had a broader concept of family.

Mary Goes to a Wedding with Jesus

There is a story that took place at the beginning of Jesus'

ministry that Mary participates in. Some say it was the first of Jesus' miracles. There have been many different interpretations, but the story says that they traveled to Cana for a wedding (Jn. 2: 1-12). Mary was at the wedding; Jesus and his disciples had also been invited. Mary worried because the wine was running out, so she told Jesus about it. This bothered Jesus and he answered his mother quite disrespectfully: "Woman, what concern is that to you and to me? My hour has not yet come." This meant, more or less, "Why should we care?" Some explain this passage by saying that the "hour" refers to Jesus' death that will occur later as a result of his ministry. Mary simply informed him of a fact, but Jesus seemed to feel that she is rushing his ministry. Jesus did not think this was the right time and so Mary received a somewhat disrespectful response, one typical of young people of that age. All mothers go through this, even Jesus' mother. What is interesting is that Mary didn't argue with Jesus (and from experience I can testify that arguments with young people are often unfruitful). She simply said to the servants, "Do whatever he tells you" (Jn. 2: 5). We see here a woman of authority, a leader giving direction for what needed to be done. Mary left the events in her son's hands. She didn't ask anything of him; she simply reported to him that there was no wine. Mary didn't get upset with Jesus' response; instead she recognized that he was a special son, and trusted that he would do what was best under the circumstances.

I've heard that people interpret stories symbolically: for example, some interpret this story so that Mary represents the faithful Israel and Jesus and his disciples represent the new community of faith. The "wine" would be the joy of the messianic era and the "vessels" the Law. That is why, when Mary stands with John under the cross, Jesus again calls her "woman" and draws her to John, her "new son" and representative of the Christian community. At the same time he shows John his "new mother." With this gesture Jesus unites the believing Jews to the Christian community. This could be a legitimate reading. However, it is also important to see in this story Mary as a woman and mother, and her relationship with others. This helps us to recognize the activity of women inside and outside the movement of Jesus.

Mary Suffers the Persecution and Execution of Her Son

Other than what I have told you, there is little more to hear about Mary. The stories tell only that Jesus' mother and brothers sought him at different times as he traveled with his followers through towns and villages. Perhaps there is no mention of Joseph because he has passed away by then. One story relates that Jesus' family thought he was not in his right mind (Mk. 3: 21) and that is why they looked for him. Mary surely must have worried about him on many occasions, as any other mother would. She would have been very aware of the danger he put himself in for speaking in public about the Kingdom of God, when for the Romans the only official Empire was theirs. Jesus did have a home in Nazareth, yet he was heard to say he had "nowhere to lay his head" (Lk. 9: 58). Maybe Mary thought he should return home to Nazareth and take care of himself. Or perhaps Mary needed him, as the firstborn son, to answer for her after her husband died as is the custom.

In any case, the conflictive situation in which Jesus and his followers moved would not have allowed Mary to live in peace. But Jesus thought otherwise. He felt Mary needed to let him go so that he could be a brother to all the world and not just to his brothers in the flesh. As brothers and sisters of Jesus, we all become children of God. Jesus had a new and different understanding of family: all those who do the will of God become brothers and sisters in this family (Mt. 12: 46-50; Mk. 3: 31-35; Lk. 8: 19-21). This is an extensive family, in which all are equal and none dominates the others. This was one important characteristic of the movement of Jesus. Mary, therefore, had to let go of being his biological mother and of her exclusive "ownership" of her son. She too had to become a member of the broader family Jesus was creating, a new community with new social and cultural values. Significantly, in the original movement founded by Jesus, the patriarchal household is rejected.

I don't really know if Mary understood this while Jesus was alive. But I can understand perfectly the pain and anguish a mother would feel witnessing her son's outspokenness and daring actions in the face of authorities who would soon seek to capture and kill him. Many stories refer to the Pharisees and Scribes who wanted to trick him in order to take him prisoner. Jesus had to flee from several places because they wanted to stone him (Jn. 10: 31; 11: 8). Undeniably Jesus *was* very daring and direct when he spoke against the authorities. But if Mary experienced anguish because of the risks her son took, she must also have felt a great deal of satisfaction and gratefulness to God for having Jesus as her son. Surely she heard about all he did—the miracles like the multiplication of the loaves of bread to feed thousands of people, the healings experienced by so many people, the casting out of demons! She must have admired the way he taught women and his attitude toward them; he treated women as no other man had before. Yes, Mary must have been proud of her son Jesus, although she may not have understood many things.

Witnessing the crucifixion of her son would have been the most painful event for Mary. Most certainly she considered everything that was happening to be completely unjust. After all, Jesus had given his entire life to fulfilling the will of God, to serving the needy. Who among us is *not* moved to tears when we recall the crucifixion of Jesus? Can we imagine what it must have been like for Mary, the one who had carried him in her womb, cared for him as a mother, and watched him from afar? For a mother to witness the death of her son gives incomparable pain. She never ceased to be his mother, and the communities continue to refer to her as the mother of Jesus.

Surely Mary was the first among those women who love and dare. Remember that she dared to remain at the cross with the other women in spite of the danger of imprisonment. She remained with Jesus, who was undesirable in the eyes of the dominant religious and political power. She was a courageous woman who went against the current in a society occupied by foreign armed forces. These forces, through Pilate, condemned her son and would try to do away with the movement of Jesus, the Messiah.

Notes

1. This is difficult to judge in Mary's case, as well as in the case of James, the brother of Jesus. We know little about him during the movement of Jesus in Palestine. It was after the resurrection that he achieved considerable importance in the community in Jerusalem to the point of being named head of that community.

2. Mercedes Navarro and Carmen Bernabé, *Distintas y distinguidas. Mujeres en*

la Biblia y en la historia (Madrid: Publicaciones Claretianas, 1995), p. 95. For the authors the greeting is typically relational.

3. Richard A. Horsley, *Galilee: History, Politics, People* (Valley Forge, Penn.: Trinity Press International, 1995), p. 193.

4. Notice that it says "the son" and not "your son." Mary the mother must even know that Jesus is not her property. She will suffer as do all mothers when Jesus begins a ministry often incomprehensible to her.

5. Bruce J. Malina and Richard L. Rohrbaugh, *Social Science Commentary on the Synoptic Gospels* (Minneapolis: Fortress Press, 1992), pp. 289-290.

6. Luise Schottroff observes the gynocentric element of the narration. It speaks of the months of gestation, the movements of the child that occur around the sixth month. *Lydia's Impatient Sisters: A Feminist Social History of Early Christianity* (Louisville: Westminster John Knox Press, 1995), p. 192.

7. Sharon Ringe points out that the body of Elizabeth teaches her "theological truths." *Luke* (Louisville: Westminster John Knox Press, 1995), p. 34.

8. Ibid., p. 34.

9. Luise Schottroff, *Lydia's Impatient Sisters*, p. 193.

10. Most exegesis emphasizes the fact that only John mentions Jesus' mother. However, a recent commentary opens up the possibility that she may also be mentioned in Mark by considering the names of James and Joseph as the brothers of Jesus and sons of Mary. See Robert H. Gundry, *Mark: A Commentary on His Apology for the Cross* (Grand Rapids: William B. Eerdmans Publishing Company, 1993), p. 977.

11. See Alois Stöger, *El evangelio según san Lucas* (Barcelona: Herder, 1979), p. 73.

12. See Sharon Ringe, *Luke*, p. 41.

13. Malina and Rohrbaugh, *Social Science Commentary*, pp. 299-301.

14. Ibid.

Chapter 2

Martha and Mary– Friends of Jesus

(Luke 10: 38-42; John 11: 1 – 12: 11)

I, Lydia, greatly appreciate the stories that include women. We have always been a part of the movement of Jesus, here and in Palestine, but when stories about Jesus are told, we are easily excluded. That is why when we hear a woman mentioned, especially by name, we prick up our ears and safely conclude that her participation must have been so important that she couldn't have been left out.[1] It's not that we have always been consciously and intentionally excluded, but the cultural tradition that does not allow women to leave the household is so strong that our exclusion seems natural.

There are several stories about Mary and Martha and their relationship with Jesus. This indicates that they were, in truth, great disciples and that they belonged to the movement of Jesus. I want to share three stories that show both how they challenged the roles imposed on women, and the strong ties of friendship between the women and Jesus. In the Scriptures the stories are told separately, but I am going to interrelate them.

Women for the Household?

Martha and Mary lived in Bethany,[2] a town about two miles from Jerusalem. There was nothing especially noteworthy about the town. It was insignificant when contrasted with the wealthy and modern city of Jerusalem. The Temple and Herod's Palace were in Jerusalem. The Palace was later occupied by the Roman procurator, Pilate, who condemned Jesus to death. Every time I hear the stories, I notice that Jesus didn't really like to go to Jerusalem; it was a dangerous city for him and his disciples because the Jewish and Roman authorities there wanted to take Jesus prisoner. But in the home of his friends Martha, Mary, and Lazarus he found refuge. Whenever he was in danger, he went either to their home or toward Samaria, to the other side of the Jordan (Jn. 10: 40) or to Ephraim, a region close to the desert (Jn. 11: 54). He seemed to enjoy visiting his friends in Bethany to spend time with them in their house and to share important things about the movement. It is interesting to note that the women appear in the stories more often than their brother Lazarus, and it seems they were more active, at least according to the stories. Jesus loved the three very much. And they were not from Galilee but from Judea, which indicates that Jesus also had people from Judea in his movement.[3]

I am convinced that Martha and Mary were disciples and followers of Jesus. I see evidence of this, for example, when Jesus visited them and sat down and began to teach them as he was accustomed to doing in Galilee with a certain circle of men and women disciples. And surely there were women disciples in this circle, even if they aren't mentioned. Mary showed great interest in everything Jesus said. She listened closely, setting aside household chores to sit at the feet of Jesus—just as the Apostle Paul sat at the feet of his famous teacher, Gamaliel, as some say (Acts 22: 3).

For Mary and other women, this was a new role. We are not permitted to study. It is deemed not fitting for us to do anything considered by our Jewish and Greco-Roman culture to be activities only for men. And in Judea, so close to Jerusalem, the spiritual center of Judaism, it is also difficult for women because of the Temple and the teachings of the scribes and priests, who hold more strictly to tradition. Jesus had a different perspective, though. There was room for women in his movement. I have also heard that the Galileans were more open with respect to the laws of the Temple.[4] Jesus, a Galilean, did not consider it a waste of time to teach Mary and Martha. He encouraged women to break out of their traditional roles of cooking, cleaning, and housekeeping. I believe he wanted them to discover new areas that would fill them with satisfaction and make them feel like whole persons with abilities similar to those of men. Jesus wanted women to participate in the movement and in local communities and to benefit. I, Lydia, believe if Jesus thought this way, then it must be that we women do have something important to contribute.

Martha, who apparently was in charge of the house, tended to busy herself with household chores (Lk. 10: 38-42). But Jesus broadened her horizon and showed her a new world in which she could move and grow, learn new things, study, discuss, and contribute. Mary had already discovered this, although the story portrays her as being very quiet, a listener. I believe that Jesus wanted Martha and all of us women to do the same—to listen and learn. And in fact, in another story we will see that Martha was a great leader. This is what allows us as women to feel that we are an important part of the movement and of our community. It isn't easy because we are struggling against a strong social current. But Jesus told Martha that the part that Mary had chosen would not be taken away from her (Lk. 10: 42). I take hold of this promise as well and have taken on the leadership of the community here in Philippi that meets in my home (Acts 16: 40).

I believe that things are changing little by little. Even the way the story is told is groundbreaking: it says Jesus went into their home without even mentioning Lazarus, who as a male would have been the homeowner, and by stating that Martha was the one who received him in her home, when the custom is for men to receive and welcome visitors. I take these things very seriously. These are elements that can change the patriarchal vision we all have of our world. Let me add, honestly, that as a woman I would have liked it even better if the three of them—Martha, Mary and Lazarus, if he was there—had taken care of the household chores together!

Martha's Confession

I'm going to tell you another story about Martha and Mary. It is the account of the death of their brother Lazarus and how Jesus raised him from the dead (Jn. 11: 1-44). It is a beautiful story. Once again the two women are the most important characters. But what is interesting here is that the one who carried on a deep theological discussion with Jesus is Martha, not Mary. Martha appears here as a wise and very active woman. She continued to be the one to receive Jesus, but this time it was not in her house. There Mary received the many who came to console them at the death of Lazarus, while Martha went out to the street to meet Jesus. Mary remained at home attending to the guests. The responsibilities were shared. Jesus didn't enter the home where they were mourning. Instead he went directly to the tomb where Lazarus had been laid. Jesus went to raise the dead man from the grave. He had the power to do such an act and he had come to bring new life.

They say that Jesus' situation was difficult; he was being sought in Jerusalem by many who wanted to kill him. The authorities thought that by getting rid of the leader of this movement they would end it and that way the Roman troops wouldn't demolish the nation (Jn. 11: 45-50). Jesus knew this, which is why he was now in a region outside of Jerusalem. When the sisters sent word that their brother was ill, Jesus decided to go to Judea. The disciples didn't want him to go and said, "Rabbi, the Jews were just now trying to stone you, and are you going there again?" (Jn. 11: 8). But Jesus decided to risk it. It was important for him to visit his friends. He wanted to give them the gift of bringing back Lazarus, their dead brother. This powerful act of restoring life to the dead hastened Jesus' imprisonment and eventual death sentence. For many believed in him as a result of this sign, and the authorities could not permit his growing power and influence. They even wanted to kill Lazarus after Jesus had raised him from the dead (Jn. 12: 10)!

When Jesus arrived in Bethany, Martha went to meet him on the road and there, the two of them, in front of the disciples, spoke about deep things. They talked about the resurrection, eternal life, the faith in Jesus that brings life eternal in spite of physical death, and other things. No doubt Martha must have asked many questions, and Jesus answered her. Martha explained what she had learned and Jesus corrected her and showed her different ways of perceiving the deep mysteries of God. In the midst of this dialogue between these friends who were also Teacher and student, Jesus revealed to her the purpose of Lazarus' death: "I am the resurrection and the life. Those who believe in me, even though they die, will live, and everyone who lives and believes in me will never die." Then he asked her an important question, "Do you believe this?" Martha answered with great faith and assurance, "Yes, Lord, I believe that you are the Messiah, the Son of God, the one coming into the world" (Jn. 11: 27). This was Martha's confession of faith. I believe that in proclaiming faith in Jesus as the Messiah, Martha was contrasting the life-giving power of Jesus with the oppressive, controlling patriarchal power. At the same time, having made the confession with her own mouth, she committed herself to the movement of Jesus as an alternative to that power.[5]

Martha's confession is often overlooked, if not forgotten. We are far more likely to hear Peter's (Mt. 16: 16) than Martha's, in spite of the fact that Martha's confession was first and far more eloquent.[6] I think that Peter's confession is remembered mostly because he is a man. Such are the prejudices of this culture that we fight against.

Truly, Martha and Mary were courageous women who loved and dared. They lived in a precarious situation. To commit themselves to the movement of Jesus, while living in Judea so close to Jerusalem, was risky. Jesus proposed many new things concerning cultural, social, and religious traditions. And there were many women and men joining the movement because they were unhappy with the political situation and wanted changes. None of this was looked upon favorably by the Jewish and Roman authorities; they had to be very careful. An example of this is when Martha, after speaking with Jesus, went to find Mary so that she too could go see Jesus and hear the words of life that Jesus had shared with her. When she arrived at the house, Mary was sitting on the floor[7] with the Jewish acquaintances who had come to comfort them. She whispered in Mary's ear that Jesus had arrived. Perhaps she whispered instead of speaking out loud because she knew about the hostility people in the region felt toward Jesus.[8] Mary then left the house without saying where she was going. The people thought she was going to the tomb to mourn her brother (Jn. 11: 28-31), but she was going to see Jesus. Perhaps she, too, had faith that Jesus could do something miraculous for her brother.

The deep friendship between Jesus and this family stands out to me. It helps me to see that the movement of Jesus was not one that sought only to change the order of things with primary concern for the difficult economic and political situation. Not only did Jesus' followers give themselves constantly to working, teaching, healing, and miracles, but they also took time to relate to each other with affection and tenderness. I see it here in Martha and

Mary's house. I can imagine that it was this way when they shared meals together in which everyone participated.[9]

The Friendship of Martha, Mary, and Jesus

I can tell by the way the stories are told that Jesus loved Mary, Martha, and Lazarus very much. In the story that I referred to before, Jesus entered the house like a member of the family and felt right at home with them. He sat down to talk with Mary, who listened attentively while Martha complained to him about taking her sister away from important chores. Jesus tenderly scolded her,[10] "Martha, Martha," he said, and counseled her to also take advantage of the opportunity to learn. This is a right that is always being taken away from us as women. We feel an atmosphere of friendship in this scene. I, Lydia, as a seller of purple cloth, leader of the Christian community, and head of my household, sometimes feel like Martha, overworked and anxious. Like Martha, I forget about my own needs, and feel that I can't get everything done. But then I remember this story. I begin to calm down and do what is within my reach, giving priority to those things that will most fulfill me as a woman, as a person of dignity. Jesus gives good advice to all women through this story of Martha and Mary!

Frequently this story (Lk. 10: 38-42) is interpreted as an instruction to divide prayer time or time devoted to being in Jesus' presence from time given to action and activities. Actually the most profound lesson of this story is that Jesus frees women from traditional roles and gives them equal opportunity to participate with the men in the movement.

In the story of Lazarus' death, Jesus' friendship with Mary, Martha and their brother can be seen most clearly. It is a very moving one. Several times we hear that Jesus loved them (Jn. 11: 5), and that he was deeply moved twice (Jn. 1: 33, 38) and shed tears for Lazarus (Jn. 11: 35), even when he knew he would be raising him from the dead. But Jesus is deeply moved by our pain—the pain of human beings. When he saw his friends crying in grief as well as the others who had come to comfort them, he was unable to hold back his own sorrow. He cried with them for the loss of his friend Lazarus. Even those who did not like Jesus said: "Look how he loved him" (Jn. 11: 36). To have a person as the leader of our movement who can love his companions—women and men—so intensely is something we must always remember. And so we must also love each other in the same way as members of the movement of Jesus, without regard for status, culture or gender, for through our faith in Christ we are indeed all made equal (Gal. 3: 28).

In this same way, the love these women felt for Jesus was immense. And he knew it. One time, near the time of the Passover and shortly before Jesus was condemned to death and crucified, his friends in Bethany held a dinner for him (Jn. 12: 1-11). Jesus arrived with some of his disciples. I'm sure they were all joyous because Lazarus, the brother who had been brought back to life, was at the meal. Martha, who appears here as the head of the household, served the meal. Then Mary expressed her love for Jesus in a very particular way. She took a costly perfume, made of pure nard, and anointed Jesus' feet with it. This was a demonstration of great love that went beyond the custom of washing a visitor's feet as a sign of hospitality. She washed Jesus' feet with a costly perfume and then dried them with her long hair.

Instantly the fragrance perfumed the entire house. Jesus had a premonition that soon the officials would kill him, which is why this gesture was one of the most meaningful expressions of love a disciple could offer him. Mary did it for her friend and teacher Jesus, probably foreseeing that she would soon be losing him. Judas Iscariot did not appreciate the gesture; he considered it a useless and wasteful act and criticized Mary. Jesus defended her and allowed Mary the pleasure of this expression of love and respect. He saw in it something beyond the simple act of foot washing. He saw in it a symbolic anticipation of the embalming of the body for burial as is our custom. The story ends by telling us that the High Priests wanted to kill him and Lazarus as well (Jn. 12: 10). Jesus allowed his disciple and friend Mary to touch his body one last time, thus sealing an eternal uninterrupted friendship with the Jesus who lived in Palestine and the resurrected Jesus. Later on, Jesus, imitating Mary's act, washed the feet of his disciples to teach them that his followers should serve others. This is a characteristic of the movement of Jesus: its purpose was to serve and not to be served.

I don't understand how it was possible for the authorities of the Christian Church in Jerusalem, the "notables" as they are called, to have forgotten Martha and Mary[11] as main characters. No one here in Philippi, or in the other provinces of the Empire outside of Jerusalem seems to know what happened to them. We only hear about James, John, Peter, and Paul, the founder of our community. That should not have happened.

Notes

1. Sharon Ringe notes that the mention of these women in two Gospels which come from different sources "testifies to the prominence of these women in the Christian tradition, especially given the many women who remain unnamed or identified only by a husband's or a father's name." See *Luke* (Louisville: Westminster John Knox Press, 1995), p. 161.

2. Luke doesn't mention the name but John does twice.

3. Zacchaeus is from Jericho in Judea.

4. Richard A. Horsley, *Galilee: History, Politics, People* (Valley Forge, Penn.: Trinity Press International, 1995), p. 277. According to this author, the institutions and traditions of Jerusalem signified a distant government for Galilee. When they developed they were under the administration of a different imperial province.

5. Mercedes Lópes describes it this way in *A Confissão de Marta. Uma Leitura a Partir de uma Óptica de Género* (São Paulo: Paulinas,1996), p. 67.

6. According to Elisabeth Moltmann-Wandel, perhaps Martha has been forgotten because she caused her contemporaries anxiety. She was a woman leader, an apostle, who was aggressive, wise and who behaved against all established conventions. She stands next to Peter in this regard. See *The Women Around Jesus* (New York: The Crossroad Publishing Co., 1982), p. 26.

7. Women sit on the floor during mourning. See Raymond Brown, *The Gospel According to John (I-XII)* (New York: Doubleday & Co., Inc., 1979), p. 677.

8. J. Mateos and J. Barreto, *El evangelio de Juan* (Madrid: Cristiandad, 1982), p. 506.

9. Suzanne Tunc believes that to be with Jesus in the movement implies partici-

pating in the meals. *También las mujeres seguían a Jesús* (Santander: Sal Terrae, 1999), p. 61s.

10. According to Alois Stöger the repetition of the name indicates sympathy, solicitude and love. *El evangelio según San Lucas*, 1979, p. 314.

11. Some believe that the two represent two kinds of church communities, those that are referred to as domestic, represented by Martha and dedicated to offer hospitality, resolve conflicts, seek unity and hold prayer meetings. The other, the missionary churches, are related to the prophets who announce the Word of God after having heard and meditated on it. If this is so, it is very significant for women because it affirms that from the origins of Christianity women have been followers of Jesus and have shared in important tasks. See Suzanne Tunc, *También las mujeres seguían a Jesús*, p. 44.

Chapter 3

The Woman
Who Was Not Stoned

(John 8: 1-12)

Now I am going to tell you another surprising story—surprising because it is about a woman caught in adultery who was not stoned as the law demanded! You might ask yourselves how this could be. Even here in Philippi under Roman law fathers or husbands can kill adulterous women caught in the act, without any kind of trial.

Well, the story probably took place during the week that Jesus was to be condemned to death. He was in Jerusalem, teaching in the Temple during the day and going to the Mount of Olives at night (see Lk. 21: 37-38).[1] The situation was tense for Jesus and his movement. His actions that reveal to us justice and mercy were considered by the authorities in Jerusalem to be completely disrespectful of the law and cultural customs. In addition, many marginalized people sought Jesus to hear him and to be healed, while others joined the movement and followed him. This was threatening in the eyes of the Romans, who were the military, political, and economic force in the region (Jn. 11: 47-48).

As I said before, there was no peace in Palestine either when Jesus lived in Galilee or today. Several movements have arisen that feed on the hopes of the people. Our history as the people of Israel speaks of a liberating God that freed the slaves when Jesus' ancestors lived in subjection in Egypt. For us, Jesus is the Son of God, and that God is the same God who liberated the people from Egypt.

So at the time when the "trial" of the woman found in adultery took place, Jesus was in a very delicate situation. The Scribes and Pharisees were seeking for a way to take him prisoner legally, and the only way they could do this was to catch him saying or teaching an untruth or something that contradicted the law of Moses. That is why Jesus left the city in the evenings and went to the Mount of Olives, next to the valley of Kidron.

The Cruelty of the Laws

Our laws against adultery are very severe, especially with respect to women. I have noticed that this is true in all cultures: the law is applied more harshly against women than against men. The problem here in the Roman provinces and in Palestine is that a woman is considered the private property of a man, be it her father or her husband. When our parents arrange a marriage, they commit us to a man of a particular family; and when we get married, we become the property of that man. So if we commit adultery we are violating our husband's private property. The problem is not one of jealousy and infidelity, but rather that both the woman and the man with whom she commits adultery have disrespected the husband's property. This concept is very clear in the Ten Commandments where it says "You shall not covet your neighbor's house; you shall not covet your neighbor's wife, or male or female slave, or ox, or donkey, or anything that belongs to your neighbor" (Ex. 20: 17). Here we women are considered as objects that belong to our husbands. Now, I am not in favor of adultery, but I certainly don't like the fact that we women are not viewed or treated as people.

In order to have a better grasp of the story, I want to tell you something about our laws. The legal system in Jerusalem follows the laws of Moses, as long as it does not enter into conflict with Roman law. Adultery (Lev. 20: 10; Dt. 22: 22-24) and blasphemy (Lev. 24: 14-16) are punishable by the death penalty which is carried out by stoning or hanging. Death by stoning is a cruel punishment; it is a slow, painful death. In those days in Palestine there was a heated debate about whether a woman caught in adultery should be punished by hanging, which is not so cruel, or by stoning. The Jews had not been able to reach an agreement on this.[2]

Here in Philippi Roman law applies. But I think it is even worse. It says that if a father surprises his daughter in adultery in his house or in his son-in-law's house, he can immediately kill her and the man with her.[3] The law of Moses is equally cruel. At least under that law for stoning to be done there must be two witnesses who catch the adulterers in the act and the accusation must be verified. When the charge is proven, the witnesses are the first to throw stones because they are responsible for the outcome of the trial (guilt or innocence); then everyone joins in the stoning.[4]

Jesus Didn't Stone the Adulterous Woman

The story begins very early in the morning with Jesus first at the Mount of Olives, and then at the Temple. We hear how all the people sought him and how he would sit down to teach them. In our culture, to sit down and teach implies authority. The story begins this way to show us the very special authority Jesus had. It was authority that was derived not from the letter of the law, as was the case with many of the Scribes and Pharisees, but from himself, "from above," they say.

Then, while he was teaching, the Scribes and Pharisees interrupted him. They had with them a woman who had been caught in adultery, whom they placed in the midst of everyone. The story doesn't tell us anything about the woman. Was she married or engaged? Perhaps she was engaged; the punishment of stoning was very clearly indicated for young women engaged to be married. The law doesn't specify the type of punishment for married women, which meant they would most likely have been punished by hanging. This is all very confusing, because in practice almost all women accused of adultery have been stoned.[5]

We know nothing about the woman's feelings, but as a woman, I can imagine that she was terrified. If it were true that she had committed adultery (sometimes a husband would set a trap when he wanted to get rid of his wife), her life was over, even if she wasn't condemned to death. Women in our culture must be very careful of their reputations in order to remain above suspicion. Otherwise, they are considered to deserve abandonment or death. Fathers worry about their daughters' reputation day and night, from the time they are children.

Getting back to the story, the Pharisees and Scribes positioned the accused woman where everyone could see and judge her. The accused man should have been with her as well, but the story doesn't mention him. (See Lev. 20: 10.) Perhaps he escaped; the law clearly places the blame on both parties involved in the act of adultery and punishment is handed out to both. I have heard of cases in which men escape or give bribes, or participate in a trap set by the husband. Many injustices are committed in these cases. Now I'm not saying the women are never guilty, but there is basic injustice behind the whole system given the fact that women are considered property, not persons. So the woman, set before everyone, is indeed the center of this story until its end.

So they said, "Teacher, this woman was caught in the very act of committing adultery. Now in the law Moses commanded us to stone such women. Now what do you say?" (Jn. 8: 4-5). It seems that they were asking what type of punishment the woman (who is assumed to be guilty for having been caught in the act) should be given—hanging or stoning. We don't hear anything about the two witnesses; perhaps she had already been tried by the Sanhedrin,* according to the law and had been found guilty. So they presented Jesus with the problem of the death sentence, since there had been an intense discussion about death by stoning. I have since heard that ultimately the Pharisees want to reduce the number of persons who would be condemned to this type of death. I hope they do, since I disagree with the death penalty, especially by stoning!

This was a very difficult and dangerous issue given the life and death situation Jesus himself was in. The question was asked of him with the intention of finding Jesus guilty of something as the woman had been (Jn. 8: 6). Both Jesus and the woman faced the possibility of death from the same legal system, although for different reasons. If Jesus said something that could be interpreted as blasphemous, he would deserve stoning according to Jewish law, as Stephen had (Acts 7). But because the question had to do with capital punishment, Jesus was in a doubly dangerous situation. A few years before, Roman law had forbidden the Jews to practice the death penalty.[6] Only under Roman law could the death penalty be applied. So Jesus was trapped. Any answer he gave could have been fatal. If he spoke in favor of stoning, he would be setting himself against Roman law and against his own practice of mercy. If he came out against stoning, he would be contradicting the law of Moses, a grave fault in the eyes of the authorities of the law. I can visualize all eyes and ears on Jesus as the crowd waited expectantly for his answer. Instead, he didn't say anything. He was very wise and understood the gravity of the situation. All he did was bend over and write[7] in the earth with his finger.

When I ask what or why he wrote, or what it meant (Jn. 8: 6-8), no one can answer. It is an enigma.* Some think, based on the prophet Jeremiah's words (Jer. 17: 13), that he was writing the guilt or the sins of the accusers. Others see it as a reference to the Roman custom of first writing the sentence, and then reading it in public. Others respond by saying it was simply the routine action of someone who was distracted. I don't believe any of this. Jesus carried out his ministry in a Jewish environment; I don't believe he was concerned with Roman legal protocols. Nor do I believe he was thinking of a quote from Jeremiah or that he was drawing distractedly. The situation was tense and his action remains an enigma.[8] It is equally interesting to note that the story mentions it twice. Sometimes I think it could have been a way of writing the law that demonstrates its flexibility; this law was not engraved in stone—inflexible and demanding killing. Instead, the law written in the dust is compassionate, law that takes into account all the elements of a situation before declaring the sentence. It is like the law written on the hearts that becomes conscience and takes into account the real lives of human beings. There is no slavery in a law that is written in the dust. I, Lydia, believe that it is important to have laws, but they must be just and compassionately human when applied.

Jesus didn't answer, perhaps because he didn't want to. Perhaps he pondered how to answer intelligently. But because they persisted, asking the same question, he got up and returned the question, placing the responsibility for sentencing in the hands of each person. He said, "Let anyone among you who is without sin be the first to throw a stone at her" (Jn. 8:7). This declaration was a stroke of genius. Jesus knew it would be impossible to find someone to carry out the death sentence; all of them were sinners. In this way Jesus saved the woman from stoning even as he saved himself from the tight spot in which he had been placed.

Jesus' reply was very important for women. We are often judged and discriminated against for almost anything by those who don't see their own, often greater, faults. Jesus had said it before: "You see the speck in your neighbor's eye but not the log in your own" (Mt. 7: 3; Lk. 6: 41).

And no one dared to throw a stone. Taking responsibility for killing someone weighs heavily on people when they are not just blindly following the law. I think that following the strict letter of the law often justifies not taking personal responsibility and also justifies murders, like putting Jesus to death on the cross, an act carried out according to the law. All those present, from the elderly to the young, saw themselves through the woman as though in a mirror; Jesus turned their eyes on themselves to see their own sinful condition. Nobody there was innocent; nobody there had the right to kill someone who was also not innocent. It seems that Jesus made them all feel like accomplices. And they all left, the story says, beginning with the elders who had more experience with life.

The story ends with a dialogue between Jesus and the woman. Everyone had gone, but she was still there, standing in the middle of the area. She could have escaped, but she chose not to. She waited for the second judgment, that of Jesus, the leader of the movement who announced the Kingdom of God and offered abundant life. Jesus questioned her, asking, "Woman, where are they? Has no one condemned you?" She said "No one, Lord" and Jesus answered "Neither do I condemn you. Go your way, and from now on do not sin again" (Jn. 8: 10). Jesus forgave her. Of all those present, he alone could have had the right to throw the first stone according to the law and to his own word. But he stood firmly against this death penalty. He preferred to offer her an opportunity to be restored by forgiveness and to live a full life with dignity in the community. Curiously, he didn't wait for her to ask for forgiveness, as we are often expected to do. Jesus forgave her with absolute confidence that the forgiveness would lead to a changed life.

Allow me to say that this story is not very popular here among the Christian communities. The male leaders don't tell it often and even hide it.[9] They don't know what to do with it because they think Jesus let this woman off too easily. However, I think this is one of the most important stories about Jesus' ministry. Not only did Jesus take the woman's side and forgive her, giving her a new opportunity for life, but he also pronounced against the unjust and discriminatory legal system. The woman knew she deserved the punishment for adultery; according to the text she was an adulteress and Jesus knew this as well. The injustice rested in a law that condemned someone to a death as horrendous as stoning. Equally unjust was that the woman alone was being punished, and that the law could be used and manipulated by those who wanted to get rid of their wives or fiancées. In this story Jesus stands against this unjust legal system.[10]

The woman accused of adultery challenges us in a different way. She challenges all of us to see ourselves as if in a mirror and not to be so quick to condemn others. She challenges us to look at our legal system from a perspective of higher justice—that of God's law of love and compassion and forgiveness.

Notes

1. Most scholars believe that this story did not originally belong in the Gospel of John; in fact, the vocabulary is totally different. In addition, it does not appear in the oldest and most important manuscripts of the Gospel. The story fits in perfectly with the synoptic Gospels, especially Luke.

2. See Xavier Léon-Dufour, *Lectura del Evangelio de Juan* (Salamanca: Sígueme, 1992), p. 247.

3. There are many different punishments depending on the circumstances. Fathers can kill their daughters and the adulterer only if found in the act in one of their houses; the husband can also do it under certain circumstances. A common punishment, especially for women of the upper class, was exile and confiscation of all property. Mary R. Lefkowitz and Maureen B. Fant, *Women's Life in Greece and Rome* (Baltimore: The Johns Hopkins University Press, 1992), p. 102.

4. The case of Susanna that appears in the Greek additions to Daniel (Dn. 13) demonstrates this process and also the possibility of false witnesses. The elder judges make up the adultery story because she would not have sexual relations with them. Deut. 17: 2-7 talks about the process for blasphemers.

5. We can observe this in Ezek. 16: 38-40.

6. This was about the year 30 A.D. See Raymond E. Brown, *The Gospel According to John (I-XII)* (New York: Doubleday & Co. Inc., 1966), p. 337.

7. The Greek word means "draw," "make lines or signs" or "write."

8. The interpretations that Lydia shares are those proposed by some current commentaries. The final alternative Lydia suggests is my [Elsa Tamez's] proposal.

9. The history of the text, although it is very old, was not recognized until much later. It was difficult for the communities to accept Jesus' forgiveness of an adulteress. Adultery was unacceptable for the baptized who could be excluded from the community and even from the love of God. Xavier Léon-Dufour, *Lectura del Evangelio de Juan*, p. 247.

10. According to Luise Schottroff, an important and seldom noted aspect of this text is the critique of the brutality of the patriarchal system against the lives of women through its power to regulate their sexuality. In the story, adultery is sin, but not a sin that is deserving of capital punishment. *Lydia's Impatient Sisters*, p. 185.

I, Lydia, seller of purple cloth and leader of the Christian community in Philippi, have noticed a very particular version of the story of the women who remained near the cross of Jesus of Nazareth. I have called your attention to the courage it takes to stay near a crucified person and that the versions of the story differ as to which women stayed at the cross. For me, the most important thing is that they were women and that they give us an example of tremendous courage. But it is curious that one of the versions of this story mentions Jesus' aunt (Mary's sister),[1] and another Mary, the wife of Clopas. I have never heard anything about these women. They are completely absent from the stories about the life of Jesus of Nazareth.[2] From experience I know that women are generally not included in the stories, except for those credited with some great achievement that is impossible to omit. It doesn't seem strange to me that Jesus would have an aunt who was also part of the movement and who would have come to Jerusalem from Galilee with the other women.

I would like to have known more about these two women. To know, for example, what motivated them to participate in Jesus' movement and what led them to be so close to their leader, so that even at the moment of his death they followed him. Could it be that the aunt risked her life only to accompany her sister? Or perhaps she and the other Mary, the wife of Clopas, wanted to be in solidarity with Jesus, their leader, as he was condemned to death on the cross.

The stories are silent concerning the existence of Jesus' aunt; they say absolutely nothing. But then, neither do they say much about Jesus' brothers and sisters, even though one of them, James, became a head of the church in Jerusalem after the resurrection. The stories are silent concerning Mary, the wife of Clopas, but neither do they say much about Clopas. But I believe these were flesh-and-blood women who were very involved in the Jesus movement.

Like them, there are many women who go unnoticed in everyday life, yet who set examples of struggle and resistance. We have much to learn from these women and it is important to mention them whenever we have the opportunity. In this second part of my witness I want to share about the women who struggle and resist.

Notes

1. See the Introduction (page 1) concerning the problem of the names and the number of women near the cross.

2. This is the only place where Jesus' aunt is mentioned (Jn. 19: 25). We know nothing about her or the wife of Clopas. A "Cleopas" appears conversing with a companion on the road to Emmaus (Lk. 24: 18), but we don't know if this is the Clopas whose wife is mentioned.

Chapter 4

Women in Two Parables

(Luke 18:1-8; Luke 15:8-10)

Up until this point I, Lydia, have told you actual stories about real women. But I have also heard many parables that Jesus told in which women are the main characters. To me these women are also very real; parables teach by using examples from everyday life.

The Widow Who Persevered Until Justice Was Done (Luke 18: 1-8)

This particular parable has to do with the struggle and resistance of a poor woman, a widow. Each time I hear the story of this widow, I find new energy to continue resisting within the context in which I live. Resistance is indispensable for those of us women who aren't satisfied with the life of submission we lead, so filled with obstacles to our fulfillment as human beings. Many of the stories of women I find in the Scriptures are highlighted by resistance and perseverance. When we resist and struggle without fainting against any injustice placed in our way, we begin to attain what we seek.

Jesus told the parable of the stubborn widow to encourage his followers to persevere in prayer and to struggle against injustice while awaiting the coming of the Kingdom of God.[1] This parable concerns the importance of praying without ceasing. Jesus assures his followers that God will do justice in the end.

The setting of this parable is a city—which city we don't

know, but here all the cities are very much alike. Understandably, they differ from the rural areas; there are many attractions and much perversion in the cities. It is well known there are authorities in the cities who are too often corrupt and seek their own interest and expect to be worshiped by the people. Frequently they make alliances with the priests, governors, military chiefs and the rich. But this is nothing new. In the writings of the Prophets we read the critiques of the kings, judges, priests and false prophets of Israel and Judah. This doesn't mean that there aren't any good people—but the corrupt certainly abound! Doesn't it seem that wherever there is money and power there is corruption?

This parable specifies that the judge was a bad character who did not fear God or respect human beings. I believe such judges are found everywhere. The insistence in the Scriptures on doing justice for the widow and orphan is due to the fact that generally, for those living in poverty, there was no justice. It was preferable to listen to those who had power, prestige and money[2] than to those who sought justice. In the parable, we hear twice that this judge respected no one, not even God (Lk. 18: 2, 4). Respect for God and human beings is part of a whole way of living: to respect our neighbor is to respect God and, by the same token, to oppress the weak is an offense to God. This is what the Scriptures teach (Prov. 14: 31).[3]

Also in that city, continues the parable, lived a widow who presented herself constantly before the judge, asking him to grant her justice. In this story we have two people living in the same city who are opposites on every level. But that is the way it is. Cities are full of contrasts; many people live at the expense of others.[4] The injustice here is structural. I can see that, because as a merchant of purple cloth I relate to all kinds of people here in the city. I know that we women must be very astute in order to avoid having others take advantage of us.

The judge represented someone who was the complete opposite of the widow. She was poor, a woman, and a widow; in other words she was vulnerable and defenseless. She had a legal case pending against someone who had wronged her. She reminds me of thousands of women today in our Greek and Roman cities, and also of our ancestors. The widow, the orphan and the foreigner are the most unprotected persons in our culture; they are frequently overlooked and their rights are denied. That is why we find that the statutes in their favor are repeated frequently in the Scriptures. For example, there is one that says: "You shall not wrong or oppress the resident alien, for you were aliens in the land of Egypt. You shall not abuse any widow or orphan" (Ex. 22: 21-22).

It is clear to me our patriarchal system is responsible for the problems experienced by widows. We women belong to the men as if we were objects, and we are not given the right to make decisions about or for ourselves. Our father or husband or oldest son is supposed to defend us. So when we are widowed, no one pays attention to us. It is expected that a man will protect us. This makes me very angry. I am very critical of cultures that oppress women and I seek to be faithful to Judeo-Christian tradition. I know that our God defends the helpless. As a foreigner and a woman here in Philippi, I love to hear in the synagogue the Scripture readings that declare that God cannot be bribed; God seeks justice for the orphan and the widow, and loves the foreigner and gives him or her bread and clothing (Deut. 10: 18).

The parable doesn't tell us what injustice had been committed against the widow. I have heard that sometimes widows have their homes violently taken away from them (Lk. 20: 47). I have known of cases of widows who have gone before a judge to claim their right to a levirate marriage, that is, to marry the brother of their dead husband, in order to give birth to sons in his name.[5] We don't know why the woman went to the judge, but surely it had to be something important for her survival, since she insisted unceasingly that he hear her petition.

I want to emphasize the widow's stubbornness and perseverance. Repeatedly she went before the judge saying, "Grant me justice against my opponent" (Lk. 18: 3). The widow was simply demanding her rights before the courts of justice. It seemed she had no other recourse for justice, because she kept going back. The judge, who was responsible for seeing that justice was done, would not hear her case. The woman's situation must have been desperate. It is very upsetting to have to go continuously to the courts, when there are many other things to be done everyday. She was sure of her rights and was not willing to give up and accept the oppression by which she was being wronged. I am familiar with the courts of the Hellenistic cities; they are depressing places for the poor and for slaves. More often than not, those who have power get their way.[6] All the comings and goings to the courts make one bitter. Apparently the non-Roman courts were similar, because injustice was prevalent among the judges under Herod's jurisdiction.

The widow persists, for perseverance is her only means for overcoming. The parable says that for a long time the judge refused to listen to her or do justice on her behalf (Lk. 18: 4). She was very stubborn. Perhaps she had decided not to stop going until she got a positive response from the judge, who finally tired of seeing her every day and listening to her same story. But not only that. Although it may sound strange, I think perhaps the judge began to be afraid of her. Here was this woman who was so sure of herself that she kept coming before him; perhaps it was becoming scandalous in the eyes of other people! Maybe he was afraid of losing his honor and becoming a public embarrassment. He even admitted that this woman was capable of hitting him in the face and giving him a black eye at any moment. If that happened, everyone would know and this would certainly affect his honor and authority. That's why one day the judge said to himself, "Because this woman keeps bothering me, I will grant her justice, so that she may not wear me out by continually coming" (Lk. 18: 5).[7] Finally she achieved her goal; her insistence and her constant demand that justice be done paid off. The judge didn't concede out of his own good will; the rights of widows did not interest him. The judge gave in because he was overcome by the widow's perseverance. The judge, an arrogant man, had to give in to the request of this poor and very stubborn widow.

The widow in this parable gives all of us a great example of how we have to keep moving in the patriarchal society we live in, no matter what the cost. We can't passively allow ourselves to be imprisoned in the roles that society assigns us, for if we do, we will lose all our battles. We cannot simply accept the injustices that are committed against us and cross our arms, cry and feel helpless. We must resist and struggle.[8] No one could have imagined that a woman like the widow would have the courage to hit the judge if he did not resolve her case. Both the woman and the judge surely were losing patience. In the end, the judge gave in because the woman would not be intimidated. In fact, he saw *her* as a threat who could lead him to public shame.

At the end of this parable Jesus exhorted his listeners to follow the example of the widow and to pray without ceasing. This meant that his followers should pray and struggle for justice day and night. For though the situation is difficult and the odds are great, and there seems no hope for change, our God, who is not like the bad judge, will respond. Jesus provides the guarantee that justice will triumph. As his followers, it is our responsibility to persist, to be stubborn in prayer, and to remain steadfastly present in the struggle for justice.

The Woman Who Won't Rest Until She Finds Something Precious She Has Lost (Luke 15: 8-10)

There is another parable similar to the last one that I am constantly reminded of in the context in which I live here in Philippi. It is about a woman who doesn't give up until she finds the coin she has lost. Although this parable is short, it teaches us many things about our sisters who live in poverty and their struggle for survival. Each time I hear it, I put myself in this woman's place. I feel her anguish as she seeks for the lost coin and then her joy when she finds it. Finally, I am deeply aware of the love of God for us as Jesus compares God to this woman.

Jesus told this parable after he'd told another one with a similar message about a shepherd who cares for 100 sheep and loses one. He searches for the one until he finds it and then rejoices. Jesus told these two parables in response to the Scribes and Pharisees who criticized him for spending time among and eating with publicans and sinners.

The publicans, or tax collectors of public funds, are Jews of little influence who answer to an administrator responsible for collecting taxes.[9] They are scorned because they collect taxes for the Roman Empire. It is commonly suspected and not unusual for them to charge more than they should and keep the difference. After all, they don't earn much, so they make their money by stealing. They are discriminated against in Jewish society because of their "impure" job, and are considered sinners. And yet Jesus did not discriminate against them and so they listened to him. I am familiar with the story of a tax collector who lived in Jericho named Zacchaeus at whose house Jesus stayed. He was converted and gave back more money and possessions to the poor and defrauded than he had stolen (Lk. 19: 2-10).

Publicans and sinners are people who lived with the stigma of inferiority. It is a terrible feeling. I know about this because I am a freedwoman, and although I bought my freedom many years ago, I am still not free of the stigma of having been a slave.[10]

Some of the Scribes and Pharisees, who considered themselves to be very holy, criticized Jesus saying, "This fellow welcomes sinners and eats with them" (Lk. 15: 2). And so Jesus told them two parables, one about the lost sheep and one about the lost coin. I'm sure you have heard the parable of the lost sheep more often because it is referred to more than the parable of the lost coin. But I want to tell you about the lost coin. Few people pay attention to the woman in this parable. When they do, they focus only on the love of God for sinners. But I like to introduce myself into the world of women and notice all the details, because in their examples I find good teachings.[11]

The parable begins, "What woman, having ten silver coins, if she loses one of them, does not light a lamp, sweep the house and search carefully until she finds it?" The story doesn't tell us how she lost the coin, but that isn't important. The emphasis is on the fact that she searched and searched until she found it.

The woman in the parable is extremely poor, even miserably so.[12] Ten drachmas is very little money. We have heard that one time Herod gave the soldiers of his army 150 drachmas and the officers received much more than that.[13] If we compare what the woman had with the reward those soldiers received we realize that it was very little. A drachma is the equivalent of a *denarius* of silver. A denarius is a day's salary for a peasant who works for someone else (Mt. 20: 1-16). With the cost of living in Palestine and here in Philippi,[14] 10 drachmas would barely be enough to survive a few weeks. That is why she searches so avidly for the lost coin: it is precious to her.

The parable goes into great detail to explain what the woman does to find her lost drachma. First she lights her lamp. That meant that her house was dark, perhaps because it was only one room without windows.[15] She would need light to search for what she had lost, since it was a small object. Afterwards, the parable tells us, she swept the house. With a palm broom she could search everywhere and get into all the corners. If the floor was rocky, as in some houses of the poor, she would hear the sound it made and find it that way.[16] And finally, the parable tells us that she searched diligently and didn't stop until she found it.

Some think that the drachma the woman lost was the adornment of coins that women wore. This would have been her dowry, and thus very important for her. Women didn't remove it even when they slept. If the parable refers to this, it would indeed be a very poor adornment.[17] But I don't think that is what she was looking for. I see this woman as typical of many who are forced to work here in Palestine and all over the world. Life is hard for men who are poor, but even more so for women. The tale that women are taken care of by their husbands is a patriarchal myth.[18] For example, to survive a person needs 200 *denarii* a year. A working father with a wife and six children would need additional income. This means that women are forced to work and give the money to their husbands. The economic contribution of the woman is necessary for the survival of the family. And if they are widows with children it is even more necessary for them to work day and night. Even worse, women receive much lower salaries than men. A woman earns half of what a man earns in a day so she needs to work twice as long and twice as hard to earn the same amount. Many children work from the time they are six years old, which is another great injustice.[19]

I am more fortunate; I don't live in conditions of such extreme need. Selling purple cloth helps me to support myself and my household. Of course, I work very hard, twice as hard as men do. What I find so appealing about the movement of Jesus is that there is respect for all persons and, even more, there is special consideration given to the marginalized. In many of the stories of the movement of Jesus and women, we see his solidarity with them. To me, Lydia, a person with a somewhat stable economic condition,[20] it is an invitation to be in solidarity with all women. Please forgive my wandering away from the story, but I think these clarifications are necessary for us to better understand the parable.

The poor woman in the parable sought the coin anxiously because it represented a part of her life. She was not a rich woman and so is not able to buy the other purple cloth, the kind I don't sell, colored with the purple dye that comes from a sea creature. That cloth is a luxury for the women in Caesar's house who have money to throw around. For them a drachma is almost insignificant. But the lost sheep and the lost coin are very valuable for those who have lost them, and thus why the parables emphasize the care and concern with which they search for them.[21]

When the woman found the coin, she was filled with joy. Her joy was so great that she invited her neighbors to celebrate with her. She said, "Rejoice with me for I have found the coin that I had lost" (Lk. 15: 9).

Perhaps for many this trivial event has little meaning, but for women of little means, to be able to ensure life through one coin is a reason for joy. The happiness of the woman overflowed after all her work in search of that which was lost, and needed, and with such good results. How sad it would have been had she not found the drachma! Her joy overflowed to the point that she felt an immense need to share it with her neighbors, who probably lived in similar conditions as she. They would have understood her situation perfectly and rejoiced with her. And so we witness a shared joy, a joy of solidarity. Even though I am in a better situation because I am a merchant, I find this parable beautiful because it invites me to be in solidarity with poor women.

After telling the parable, Jesus shared a beautiful application of it. He compared the woman's joy—and the joy of the shepherd who found his lost sheep—to the joy God shares with all the angels when one of the "lost," called a sinner (people like the publicans and the marginalized) responds to the life-changing message of good news of Jesus and his movement. With this parable Jesus challenged the Scribes and Pharisees to see the publicans and sinners as God sees them—in a different light,[22] as persons of worth. As an unbeliever converted to Christianity and a freedwoman, I give thanks to God for God's solidarity with the poor and with those who are stigmatized by our patriarchal society!

Notes

1. The evangelist Luke narrates this parable conscious of the delay of the *parousia*, seeking the perseverance of the communities. Luke places the parable after the eschatological mention of the days of the Son of Man.

2. These were the three fundamental characteristics for belonging to the upper classes of society within the orders of senators, knights, and decurions. However, they also hold true for societies of the Middle East such as Israel, as we deduced from the critiques of the prophets. Actually, today's reality is not too far from this tendency.

3. See also Prov. 17: 5; 15: 25; 19: 17; 22: 22-23.

4. Marked contrasts are evident in Rome, and therefore in all the Hellenistic cities. Although the narrator Lydia speaks of her everyday experience in a Hellenistic city outside of Palestine, the same can be said to be true of the Hellenistic cities of Palestine. There were many of them in the time of Jesus. See Joaquin Gonzalez Echegaray, *Arqueologia y evangelios* (Estella: Verbo Divino, 1994), p. 45.

5. In the Hebrew Bible (Genesis 38) we read of the case of Tamar. She doesn't go to the judge but disguises herself as a prostitute to conceive with her father-in-law and have descendants; something similar happens in the case of Ruth and Boaz. If the judges won't listen, women must use their "wiles" to see that justice is done.

6. The Roman legal system was dual, with courts for the rich and noble and others for the poor. The penalties were also different, harsh for the poor and slaves, and lenient for those of the upper levels of society. See Elsa Tamez, *The Amnesty of Grace: Justification by Faith from a Latin American Perspective* (Nashville: Abingdon Press, 1993), p. 56.

7. The Greek word *hypopiazein* is strong and means to slap, lit. "hit in the eye." It is a term taken from boxing; cf. J. Fitzmyer: "Lest she come and give me a black eye" (*The Gospel According to Luke, X-XXIV* [New York: Doubleday, 1985], p.179). The versions generally soften the term and translate "bother" or "wear out my patience." Ivoni Richter Reimer translates it as a slap and talks about the patriarchal fear of slapping: "El poder de una protagonista. La oración de personas excluidas," *Revista de Interpretación Bíblica Latinoamericana* (RIBLA), no. 25 (1997), p. 62.

8. Luise Schottroff's analysis of the same parable emphasizes resistance as well and shows that the critique of women's roles is closely related to the critique of an unjustly structured economic society; without the first there is no real libera-

tion. *Lydia's Impatient Sisters*, p. 110.

9. X. Léon-Dufour, *Diccionario del Nuevo Testamento* (Madrid: Cristiandad, 1977), p. 24.

10. See Irene Foulkes, *Problemas pastorales en Corinto* (San José: DEI/SBL, 1996), p. 48.

11. The best analysis of this parable that I am aware of is Luise Schottroff's in which she analyzes the economic situation of this poor woman and her struggle for survival. My rereading of this parable is based on her research. *Lydia's Impatient Sisters*, pp. 91-100.

12. The parable of the lost sheep can also be the parable of a salaried shepherd who earns a denarius or drachma a day and searches desperately for the lost sheep because it isn't his. Ibid., p. 91.

13. J. Fitzmyer, *The Gospel According to Luke*, p. 1081.

14. The price of bread was very high, more than the grain. Those who were poor and without land had to purchase almost everything they needed. Schottroff, *Lydia's Impatient Sisters*, p. 96.

15. Joachim Jeremías, *Las parábolas de Jesús* (Estella: Verbo Divino, 1970), p. 166.

16. Ibid.

17. Ibid.

18. Schottroff, *Lydia's Impatient Sisters*, p. 95.

19. Ibid., pp. 93-95.

20. Concerning Lydia's economic situation, see the section on Lydia and Priscilla in chapter 9.

21. Sharon H. Ringe, *Luke* (Louisville: Westminster John Knox Press, 1995), p. 205.

22. Ibid.

Chapter 5

The Woman Who Stole
a Miracle From Jesus

(Mark 5: 21-43)

The System of Purity and Impurity

I, Lydia, have begun, little by little, to overcome many of the patriarchal elements of the Greco-Roman culture that marginalize me as a woman. It hasn't been easy, because cultural traditions are accepted as being the natural state of things and therefore impossible to change. But the newness of the message of Jesus the Christ, the Jew from Galilee, has propelled many of us women and many men to change our attitudes and practices. Admittedly, this has been a little more difficult for the Jewish women of Jerusalem than for the Jewish women of Galilee, since the latter are not so attached to the precepts of the Jerusalem Temple.[1] Even less attached to religious precepts are the poor women. The Pharisees, however, who live in all of Palestine including Galilee, put heavy emphasis on all precepts, especially those concerning purity and impurity. Perhaps that is why Jesus referred often to these issues. From what I have heard, Jesus stepped back from strict adherence to these precepts and criticized the Scribes and Pharisees who wanted to impose them on the entire population.

Being so close to Jerusalem and the Temple with its priests makes it more difficult in Palestine, more so than here in Philippi, for women to free themselves from the religious norms of the system of purity. That is why, when I hear a story like the healing of the woman with a hemorrhage and how she was reincorporated into society, I thank God for having shown us new ways through Jesus.[2]

To better understand the story of this sick woman, it is important that I first tell you something about the cultural and religious system in which she lived. I am very familiar with it because I was a convert to Judaism before becoming a part of the movement of Jesus, the Christ.[3]

In the society where Jesus lived, as is true today as well, daily living was organized according to a system of purity.[4] This means that all behavior is characterized by what is considered to be pure and what is considered to be impure. Anything that does not fit into a specific way of seeing things is considered to be impure. We are supposed to maintain ourselves as pure and avoid the impure and that which is dirty. People can be pure or impure. For example, pagans and Samaritans are considered to be impure. Cadavers are also impure, as well as sick persons and menstruating women. Objects can also be impure, such as a utensil touched by someone who is impure, or certain kinds of food. Places are impure—the house of a pagan, for example, or a pagan city. The Temple is pure, and days such as the Sabbath and religious feasts are considered to be sacred and must be kept without exception. There are also a whole series of detailed rules about how people and things can be purified, for example, washing one's hands up to the elbow before eating, or bathing after passing through an impure place. The law stipulates all the things that cannot be done on the Sabbath. This complicated system was not always accepted or practiced by Jesus. He was criticized for not keeping the law when he healed on the Sabbath, did not wash his hands according to the rules, and went into the homes of people considered to be impure. The Pharisees, who are so rigorous in keeping the precepts of the law, found his behavior unacceptable.

For women as well as for all poor people, this system of purity has many disadvantages. Women who menstruate each month, or who give birth and bleed for several days, are considered impure and must constantly submit themselves to rules of purification. Impure persons are separated from the community. Mary, for example, was impure for 40 days after giving birth to Jesus. To purify herself at the end of the 40 days, she had to buy two turtledoves, which were the cheapest, and offer them as sacrifices (Lk. 2:

21-24). Imagine what a woman with a chronic hemorrhage faced! The story I am about to tell you is about a woman with this disease.

This story is told often,[5] and it is always told in the context of another story. Jesus was actually on his way to heal a little girl, the daughter of a synagogue leader named Jairus. The story took place along Jesus' way; then the text continues with the story of Jairus' daughter. This occurrence is unplanned like many women's stories, and yet it has satisfactory results because a woman dared to take risks. These stories, like so many others, range from everyday occurrences to extraordinary ones. Sometimes they are made known, and sometimes not. They occur as a parenthesis of life that continues on. Because of Jesus, this particular story did not remain hidden.

The "Stealing" of a Miracle

The story begins with Jesus' return in a boat to the shore of the lake. He had been to the other side, a Gentile region in Gerasa or Gadara[6] where he had cast out many demons from a person in that place (Mk. 5: 1-20). When he returned he found a great multitude of women and men waiting for him. All of them wanted to get close to him, probably to be healed or to listen to his words. They were beautiful, for he talked about life, a new and better life for everyone. And so the poor and needy followed him everywhere. He was also sought by some people who had more elevated social positions, such as Jairus. They saw in him someone who responded equally effectively to concrete needs and so saw in the movement of Jesus a viable alternative. When Jesus spoke of the Kingdom of God, of the poor as blessed, and when he criticized the oppression and burdens of the religious system, surely people dreamed of a better world. The movement of Jesus, the Christ, was very attractive to many in Palestine. Two of the versions of this story (Mk. 5: 21; Lk. 8: 40) stress that many people followed him.

Jairus had begged Jesus to go to his house and put his hands on his daughter who lay dying. Jesus made his way there. Many people followed Jesus, so many that they almost smothered him. Among the multitude was a woman. The story doesn't tell us her name, so she remains anonymous, a woman of the people.

This woman suffered from a disease that had made her hemorrhage for many years. It was a serious condition. Women know that to lose blood is to lose life. This woman was slowly dying. But that was not the worst of it. In our Jewish culture, because of her disease, she was considered to be impure. That meant that she had to be isolated from the community and could not touch anybody. Anyone and anything she touched would become impure. She was not able to share her life with others in any way. Similarly, no one was to let themselves be touched by her lest they become impure. More than a physical sickness, then, she had a social disease.[7] Sexual relations were out of the question due to her impure state, and so she was unable to have children. Her sickness resulted in sterility as well, another powerful stigma against women. I can imagine that as a person, she was far more affected by her condition of permanent social marginalization than by the actual disease itself. She paid a heavy price for her illness; aside from suffering physically, she suffered the emotional effects of being socially marginalized. Because she was sick, she was considered a sinner, since in this cultural/religious system, sickness and sin go hand in hand. That is why when Jesus healed, he usually declared to the healed person before everyone: "Your sins are forgiven."

We know that this woman had suffered much. She had made great efforts to overcome her situation, consulting with every doctor available, but none had been able to cure her. Because of the expense involved, only the wealthy can afford physicians. The poor seek out traditional healers. The story tells us she had spent all she had on doctors but without any success. In fact, her condition was worse, and now she was poor. It's possible she was a widow who had started off with some money but was pushed into poverty by her disease. For in our culture a woman has no possessions of her own, unless she is a widow. Yet this anonymous and impure woman, lost among the multitude that pressed against Jesus, had incredible faith. She believed that just by touching Jesus' garment she would be healed and her life would change dramatically.

I believe that this woman's stubborn persistence is worthy of our attention. In spite of having exhausted all possibilities within her reach, she continued to struggle. She would not accept her situation of physical and social marginalization. Quite possibly she always considered herself to be a worthy person who deserved good health. She sincerely wanted to be healed and saw a possibility in Jesus, perhaps the best possibility, because she had heard about the people he had healed. But she didn't ask directly, as Jairus had. Perhaps she felt she didn't have the right to as a woman, especially given her state of impurity that kept her from having contact with people. Or perhaps she felt it wouldn't be appropriate to interrupt Jesus as he made his way to the house of a respectable man to do him a favor. But I think that her belief in the healing power of Jesus was so great that she was sure that just touching his clothing would heal her. Many healers had this power and, having heard much about Jesus' miracles, she would believe that he had that power as well.

The story tells us that she came up to Jesus from behind, hiding among the people. Then she touched his garment. At that very instant she felt that she had been healed. Her action was considered very bold in the context of Jewish culture. In spite of being in an impure state, she dared to touch a man and thus break the law of purity. But thanks to that boldness she was finally healed and restored to society. She was once again considered to be a worthy person. This is a great lesson for all women. In a society where the culture marginalizes us, we must act boldly and go against prevailing customs in order to challenge and change the system of discrimination.

Suppose the story had ended here. The woman was healed, nobody would have noticed, and Jesus could have continued on his way to the house of the synagogue leader. But it didn't end here; there is something else for us to learn from this story. The problem with the woman's situation was that she wanted to wrest a healing from Jesus without his knowing it. Had this happened, the overall results would not have benefitted the movement of Jesus or her or other women marginalized by the laws of purity and impurity.

Jesus Gave the Woman Dignity (Jesus Dignified the Woman)

It was very important for the multitude with Jesus to know that the woman was healed when she touched Jesus' garment, and equally important to realize that he was not made impure by the touch of a woman who had an issue of blood. And it is significant that it was made known that, although she had violated the precepts of the law, she was healed—thanks to the boldness of her transgression! If we tell boldly the actions of this daring woman, other women will also courageously dare to change the patterns of society that oppress and marginalize them. Yet, when Jesus responded, he had no intention of making himself known as a shaman or a sorcerer, for there were plenty of these. He was far more than a sorcerer. Jesus wanted the people, especially those who were marginalized, including the women, to build a new way of life and new relationships. If we act only in secret, it would be difficult indeed to change oppressive systems.

When this story is told, do you notice Jesus' insistence on discovering who had touched him? He felt power flow from him at the same time that the woman felt she had been healed. How interesting this is! Although there was almost a clandestine relationship between Jesus and the woman, Jesus knew someone had touched him and he was determined to find out who it was. Jesus stopped along the road on his way to Jairus' house and had no intention of continuing until he found the responsible person. His work would not be complete if a healing was given in hiding. He asked the crowd, "Who touched my clothes?" (Mk. 5: 30). To the disciples, who often seemed to have a hard time understanding Jesus, the Master's question seemed senseless. They said to him, "You see the crowd pressing in on you; how can you say 'who touched me?'" (Mk. 5: 31). Jesus didn't bother to answer, but continued to seek out the person who had dared to "steal" healing from him without his consent.

The woman had no other alternative but to confess. She stood up, breaking her anonymity and with fear and trembling, knelt before him, just as the synagogue leader had done. Then, in front of everyone, she told the whole truth: her past life, how she had suffered and how she came to be in her current situation. This was another critical step for the woman to take. She publicly told of her suffering and marginalization.

It was risky! The woman didn't know what was going to happen. Would Jesus get angry for what she had done? Would she be returned to her previous state of sickness? She simply confessed her action. But Jesus didn't reproach her. I don't think Jesus was concerned about having been robbed of some of his healing power. Rather, I think he wanted to show the way to a new life. He needed to demonstrate that he was not a sorcerer with a temporary cure. He wanted this woman who had been marginalized by her impurity for so many years to be restored to dignity once again, and to be an example for many. That was why he called her "daughter," a word that included her in family and implied affection. With this word he reintegrated her into society. And so she was purified, not by rites of purification, but rather with faith that empowered her to transgress the law of purity. Most importantly, her faith brought her healing and saved her from the physical and social disease that confined her. Jesus says, "Daughter, your faith has made you well; go in peace, and be healed of your disease" (Mk. 5: 34). This was a woman who struggled and resisted and regained wholeness of life.

Notes

1. R. Horsley, *Galilee: History, Politics, People* (Valley Forge, Penn.: Trinity Press International, 1995), p. 235.

2. It is interesting that this story and others obviously related to the system of purity and impurity are set in Galilee where supposedly the population was less attached to the precepts and the Temple. The fact that Jesus, who moved about almost exclusively in Galilee, made frequent reference to the laws of purity and impurity may be a sign that during his time and later, in the communities that received the Gospel accounts, this was an important topic. It is vital for women to take notice of Jesus' critique of this system since even today there are women who because of their menstruation, for example, are considered or consider themselves to be "impure."

3. It is likely that Lydia continued to attend the synagogue as a God-fearer.* At this time the division between Judaism and Christianity did not yet exist.

4. The facts that follow are taken from Bruce J. Malina and Richard L. Rohrbaugh, *Social Science Commentary on the Synoptic Gospels* (Minneapolis: Fortress Press, 1992), pp. 222-224.

5. It appears in the first three Gospels.

6. Mark and Luke read "Gerasa" while Matthew reads "Gadara," with "Gerasa" being less likely since it is a region quite removed from the Sea of Galilee.

7. According to Malina and Rohrbaugh, anthropologists distinguish between a disease of the organism and a sickness. The latter is a social issue; it has to do with a devalued state of the being itself. *Social Science Commentary*, p. 210.

Chapter 6

The Syrophoenician Woman Who Argued With Jesus

(Mark 7: 24-30; Matthew 15: 21-28)

I, Lydia, listen carefully to all the stories about the women who were related to Jesus in some way, whether or not they were a part of his movement. It's important for me to hear these accounts. Through them, I learn more about the life of Jesus, especially his acts of boldness and courage in the face of cultural norms that oppress women. Because I am a leader of the movement of Jesus, the resurrected one, to hear of his boldness gives me courage to do the same here in the provinces of the Roman Empire.

I want to tell you a story I have heard told two different ways (Mk. 7: 24-30; Mt. 14: 21-28) about a Syrophoenician woman. This story interests me because people from here, from Philippi, or people from places outside of Palestine, would probably not have been able to participate in the movement of Jesus if his message had been limited to Palestine and to the Jews. It seems that initially Jesus dedicated himself to announcing the Kingdom of God to the Jews only; he sought a profound renewal among his people, but no more. The majority, if not all of the people involved in his movement in Galilee and Judea, were Jews. For Jesus it seemed natural to dedicate his life to the people of Israel, or as the story itself says to "the lost sheep of the house of Israel" (Mt. 15: 24). But this Syrophoenician woman, whose name we don't know (referred to only as the Syrophoenician or "Canaanite" woman [Mt. 15: 22], "a woman, a Gentile, of Syro-Phoenician origin" [Mk. 7: 26]) made Jesus change his mind and made it possible for others who were not Jews to benefit from his transforming power.

This story, which is quite different from most of the other stories, made it possible for the justice of God, as our brother Paul of Tarsus says, to be revealed to all people and not just to the Jews. Today, 20 years after the death of Jesus, his movement has spread throughout many cities of the empire outside of Palestine. I, Lydia, for example, am a Gentile converted to Judaism and to the Gospel of Jesus Christ, and the brothers and sisters in faith gather at my house (Acts 16: 40). There are also God-fearing people (converts to Judaism) who like me are Gentile or pagan, as the Jews so unfortunately call us. The conservative branch of Judaism in Jerusalem refers to the Jews of the Diaspora* as Hellenistic because they live outside of Palestine. They don't consider them to be very pure because they have mixed with impure people, that is, with pagans. In addition, for many years now the Jews have not spoken Jesus' mother tongue, Aramaic. Those who can read the Scriptures do so in Greek (the Septuagint)[1] since the Jews in Palestine don't read the Hebrew in which the original Scriptures were written. Only the rabbis and a few other people, mainly men, can read the Hebrew Scriptures. When Paul writes letters to the community at Philippi and other communities, he writes in the common Greek and someone who knows how to read reads the letter before the whole community. This is how it has to be because so few people can read. Paul, a Jew of the Diaspora, was born in Tarsus, which is why he speaks Greek well. Perhaps this is also why he is concerned that those who are not Jews also be considered children of God as the Jews are.

I believe that the values of equality and compassion that are so present in the movement of Jesus made it possible to see the benefits of people other than Jews to hear the Good News. That is why we have this story in which Jesus is challenged by a Gentile woman who needs the power of Jesus to heal her daughter. This woman, the first advocate for the Gentiles, should be recognized as the first woman apostle from among the Gentiles.[2]

I like this story because it is about a very daring woman, perhaps the most daring of all the women that I have heard about in the stories of the movement of Jesus. She breaks with many of the cultural norms to find what she seeks, driven by love for her daughter.

Boundary Problems

The story tells us that Jesus went to Galilee to the region of Tyre (and Sidon). He had been in Gennesaret, on the shores of the lake, and had argued with the Pharisees. They criticized him and his disciples for not washing their hands before they ate (see Mk.7: 1-22). The washing of hands up to the elbow before eating was part of the ritual of purification in the Jewish culture, but neither Jesus nor his disciples adhered to it. As I have mentioned, it seems that outside Jerusalem people aren't as strict about following the law as they are in Jerusalem, and this may be true. But I believe that these rituals were of secondary importance to Jesus. It was more important to show compassion to the needy and to be pure in heart. He considered the experts in the law to be hypocrites who were more concerned with these outward things than with the greatest commandment–to love God and one's neighbor. After this discussion Jesus decided to go to Tyre, a Gentile region.

I need to mention that the relationship between the Syrophoenicians and the Galileans was not very good. This region on the border between Tyre and Galilee is an area of conflict. Tyre, a rich and important city, has always been famous for its maritime commerce. The purple dye of the rich is sold there, and the city is well known for its metallurgy. Galilee was economically disadvantaged in contrast to Tyre. Tyre seemed to have exploited rural Galilee and taken advantage of its agricultural products.[3] I have heard that the Jews who lived in that region were not treated well. Yet the Jews also looked down on the Syrophoenicians for mistreating them and for being pagans and impure, according to Jewish tradition. So we are talking about two peoples with two cultures living next to each other who don't get along.[4]

But in spite of this tension, Jesus decided to go to the region of Tyre. Apparently he didn't get to the city but stayed on its outskirts. One account tells that he traveled with his disciples (Mt. 15: 23) and another doesn't mention them, stating just that he went (Mk. 7: 1). It seems, in any case, that he didn't want it to be known. His fame had spread throughout Galilee and he was sought out for healings and teachings. Perhaps Jesus needed to rest and so went to a place that was not familiar to him. When he wanted to be alone, he entered a house to retreat and have some privacy.

But as the story goes, he was unable to remain unnoticed in

spite of many precautions. This would indicate that the miracles he had done in Galilee were being made known in non-Jewish territories. It was here that a woman who had heard about him came to plead for her daughter who was possessed by an evil spirit. She went into the house and knelt at his feet. In our culture this is a gesture of humility toward someone of greater rank in order to ask for a favor.[5] Kneeling before him, she begged him to heal her daughter by casting out the evil spirit. The other version of the story (in the Gospel of Matthew) says that she was a Canaanite woman; perhaps this was stated to reinforce the fact that it was a non-Jew[6] who cried to Jesus, "Have mercy on me, Lord, son of David!" (Mt. 15: 22).

Jesus Refused to Heal a Gentile Girl

What surprises me, Lydia, in both versions of the story is that Jesus didn't want to heal the girl. This attitude seems very strange knowing that Jesus was the most merciful and compassionate of all people. Surely the point is to tell us something more about the woman and, above all, about Jesus. Here's the Gospel of Matthew account. Jesus refused the woman three times. The first time he didn't answer. The disciples then asked him to tell her to leave, to give her what she asked so she would stop being such a bother. She was yelling and creating a commotion that they considered embarrassing. It seems to me that they wanted Jesus to heal the girl just so the mother would leave them alone, not because the girl was suffering. Sometimes I think that the disciples had very closed minds; it seems that they were often described that way in the stories (Mk. 5: 30-31; 6: 52; 9: 33-34; Lk. 22: 45, 49-51; Jn. 4: 31-33).

The second time, Jesus gave a negative response. He said he had been sent only to the lost sheep of the house of Israel (Mt. 15: 24). The mother insisted, begging him to help her; Jesus refused for a third time, using the well-known proverb that expresses prejudice against non-Jews. He said, "It is not fair to take the children's food and throw it to the dogs" (Mt. 15: 26).

It is clear from this story that at first Jesus denied healing to someone who was not from Israel. We see Jesus acting like very conservative and traditional Jews who believed that only Jews, those of the "household," have a right to the "bread of God." The rest—the "dogs," those from outside the household—do not.[7]

This was an unusual attitude for Jesus. He always showed himself to be compassionate and very open to the needs of others. Here is a woman who has a great need and, after all, he had just discussed issues of purity and impurity with the Pharisees, criticizing their restrictive beliefs strongly (Mk. 7: 1-23). Of all people, I would have expected Jesus to listen to her, even if she was a Gentile. And so I insist that the story must have a very important purpose, especially for women and for the Christian communities where we are leaders.

In another shorter version of this story (Gospel of Mark) Jesus didn't refuse the woman's request three times, nor was his reply overtly negative. He simply responded with the same proverb. In this version, he adds a phrase that seems to indicate that there was room for non-Jews to be blessed by the Kingdom, but only after the Jews had been blessed. It was an issue of sequence—first the Jews, then everyone else. Jesus said, "Let the children be fed first, for it is not fair to take the children's food and throw it to the dogs" (Mk. 7: 27).

The most interesting thing about this story, however, is the woman's answer to Jesus' clear refusal. In fact the most important thing about this story is the dialogue between Jesus and this nameless woman, and how it takes shape.[8] I don't think the emphasis is on the miracle, because it happens at the end and at a distance,[9] and is not given much attention. So here we have a woman who enters into strong discussion with the leader of the Galilean movement as she questions his limited perspective of responding only to those of his own culture.

The Woman Who Argued With Jesus

Who was this woman who was capable of carrying on such a difficult dialogue with Jesus finally to achieve what she wants? The story gives great detail in its description of the woman. We know she was of Greek culture, a pagan, and from Syrophoenicia. The fact that she was of Greek culture possibly means that she was not a poor woman, since those belonging to this culture were generally of more privileged social status than others. Her daughter didn't sleep on a cot, but on a bed; this too seems to indicate a more elevated social class than that of Jesus, a Jewish artisan-peasant from Galilee.[10] Of course we can't be sure of this.[11] What we can be sure about is that this woman is from a culture different from Jesus'; that she was alone and did not have help from her family, and that her daughter was born in a society in which daughters are not as appreciated as sons.[12] She was also a very stubborn woman, and a fighter. The woman had a sick daughter whom she loved. She was ready and willing to do anything for her to be healed. She had heard of a person who had the power to heal and looked for him until she found him. When she heard he was in her region, she sought him out. Her arrival was not timely; she interrupted Jesus when he was trying to remain secluded and alone. When dealing with life-and-death issues of loved ones, we as women sometimes have to do even the impossible. She dared to bother Jesus with her need. Clearly both Jesus and the disciples rejected her, but she persisted. She was stubborn and it was this very stubbornness that saved her daughter. She could have given up each time Jesus refused to answer her request. But she didn't. Because of her insistence, she got his help. She was convinced that if she were able to wrench a healing word or touch from Jesus, her daughter would be saved from the evil spirit.

This woman, perhaps important and of certain social status, didn't mind throwing herself at Jesus' feet to beg, or being rejected one, two, or three times. She insisted on Jesus' attention, knowing this was perhaps the best alternative for her daughter to be healed, perhaps her last chance. She struggled and defied all the rules by speaking to a Jewish man in the street and persisting even when his answer was negative. She didn't care that Jesus was poor and belonged to an inferior culture in the eyes of the Greeks. She swallowed her pride when he called her a "dog," thus excluding her from the benefits of the kingdom.[13] She stood firm and was able to overcome Jesus' initial negative reaction. I believe that this woman's faith (in Matthew) and the way she carried out her dialogue with Jesus (in Mark) led Jesus to change his mind and extend his hand of compassion and healing to non-Jewish peoples.

The story tells us that when Jesus responded to her with the proverb, the woman answered back with the same proverb by giving it new meaning: "Sir, even the dogs under the table eat the children's crumbs" (Mk. 7:28). This intelligent and challenging answer surprised Jesus. But the woman's sick daughter needed Jesus' healing power now. Later, after the children were fed, would be too late.

The first time I heard this story I felt sorry for that poor woman and for so many others. They seem to have to bow and scrape to get what they want. But then I thought that this is a strategy women use when we don't have the power necessary to reach our goal.[14] The table is abundant; there is food for everyone.[15] The woman changes the times; she doesn't want to wait for some to benefit and then others. She feels that, at the same time, all persons and all peoples should participate in the mercies of God.

Jesus Learned from the Syrophoenician Woman

Jesus was surprised at the woman's answer and at her faith that he could heal her daughter, and now, at her conviction that other people also have the right to participate in the Kingdom of God that he has been announcing. With her intelligence, her skill in carrying on a dialogue with Jesus, and her insistence that healing be available for all, she was able to change Jesus' position. As a result, he healed her daughter.[16] "For saying that, you may go–the demon has left your daughter." And when the woman arrived home she found that her daughter had been freed of the evil spirit and was lying in bed, healed.

This story shows me that the words of women also have power. Note how Jesus says to her: "for saying that," or "for what you have said." The faith of women can also achieve changes in spite of many obstacles. In the Gospel of Matthew the story says, "Woman, great is your faith! Let it be done for you as you wish." This story teaches me that as women we must be daring and defiant when we know that what we seek is just and for the good of many. And we need to persist when seeking justice, regardless of whom we are confronting, for stubborn determination can change rules, conduct, customs, and attitudes that marginalize people. I believe that this is one of the most profound insights that we as women can gain from the stories of other women who, in one way or another, came into contact with Jesus and his movement.

We must pay close attention to Jesus' attitude. Although he was a man and Jewish, he dared to listen to the words of a person who was not only a woman, but from another religion and culture. In spite of being a man, Jewish, and a peasant, he listened to a cultured woman who humbles herself at his feet. He did not humiliate her further by taking advantage of her to get back at those who wronged his people as had the powerful economic class of Tyre and Sidon. At first, Jesus rejected her and insulted her, but he had the courage to recognize his mistaken position. His attitude changed when confronted with the needs of Gentiles. Because of her courage and determination, we could say that this woman was a pioneer in opening the way for all peoples of the earth to benefit from the mercy of God. We can only hope that the leaders of our faith communities will follow Jesus' example; perhaps they, too, won't be afraid to change their position when the needs of our neighbors demand it. The Apostle Paul calls us to be led by faith and not by the law or tradition that so often makes us behave inhumanely.

Equally important is that Jesus listened to the pleas of the determined woman and cured her daughter as a result of her persistent arguments. Yet Jesus didn't demand that she follow him or that she become a part of the movement. He allowed her freedom to choose, in respect for her beliefs. She returned home, and Jesus left the region of Tyre and returned to Galilee. And so in all these stories I see that we learn not only from Jesus and his courage, but from the women of courage as well.

Notes

1. The Hebrew Bible was translated into Greek in the third century B.C.E. The Greek translation is called the Septuagint or LXX.

2. Cf. Schüssler Fiorenza, *In Memory of Her: A Feminist Theological Reconstruction of Christian Origins* (New York: The Crossroad Publishing Co., 1994), p. 186.

3. Cf. Gerd Theissen, *Colorido local y contexto historico de los evangelios. Una contribución a la historia de la tradición sinóptica* (Salamanca: Sígueme, 1997), p. 88.

4. Silvia Regina de Lima Silva points out: "The hostility of the Tyrians toward the Jews was manifested in permanent attacks on various territorial regions, embargo of the goods of Jews in Tyre, making part of the population slaves, and other measures that are told particularly in the writings of Josephus. We can

suppose that the Jews responded to this situation with a lack of trust and equal prejudice. "Desde debajo de la mesa: un análisis exegético de Marcos 7: 24-39." Master's Thesis, Universidad Bíblica Latinoamericana, 1999, p. 93.

5. See Bruce J. Malina and Richard L. Rohrbaugh, *Social Science Commentary on the Synoptic Gospels* (Minneapolis: Fortress Press, 1992), pp. 235-37.

6. Matthew's version seems to regard the woman as a pagan who was living among the people of Israel, which is why she recognizes Jesus as the son of David.

7. Xavier Pikaza understands the "dogs" to be those who are outside the household, separated from the table (the Gentiles), and the "children" (the Jews) to be within the household. *Pan, casa, palabra. La iglesia en Marcos* (Salamanca: Sígueme, 1988), p. 190.

8. See Jim Perkinson's interesting article about the word of the woman in "A Canaanitic Word in the Logos of Christ, or the Difference the Syrophoenecian Woman Makes to Jesus" in *Semeis*, no. 75, 1996.

9. This text has been shown to be not a miracle text but a teaching dialogue. See Joachim Gnilka, *El evangelio según Marcos* (Salamanca: Sígueme, 1992), p. 338.

10. Ibid, p. 342.

11. Silvia Regina de Lima Silva leaves the social position of the woman as ambiguous and places the emphasis on the racial conflict. "Desde debajo de la mesa," p. 102.

12. See Sharon Ringe, "A Story of a Gentile Woman," in *Feminist Interpretation of the Bible*, ed. Letty Russell (Louisville: Westminster John Knox, 1993), p. 70.

13. Jim Perkinson observes the complexity of the inferior-superior paradigm between this woman and Jesus with respect to gender, ethnicity, culture, and religion. "A Canaanitic Word in the Logos of Christ," p. 68.

14. Silvia Regina de Lima Silva rejects an interpretation of resignation and submission. For her, the woman's response manifests profound strength and energy capable of withstanding adversity and concentrating on what was essential at

that moment. "Desde debajo de la mesa," p. 104.

15. See Xavier Pikaza, *Pan, casa, palabra*, p. 190.

16. See Sharon Ringe, "A Story of a Gentile Woman," p. 71.

Part III:
Women Teachers and Disciples

I, Lydia, know well that when I hear stories about the disciples and followers of Jesus, there were women present among them. Because our language is dominated by masculine words and images, women generally aren't mentioned. We know that in our patriarchal culture the presence of women is taken for granted.[1] Proof of this is that those who tell the stories of Jesus' death, burial and resurrection felt obligated to mention the women explicitly. After all, they were the only ones present! There was no way to avoid saying clearly that these women followed and served Jesus in Galilee.

When Jesus was taken prisoner, we learn that all the disciples, men and women, fled and hid in Jerusalem. Later, when he was crucified and buried, we learn that only the women appeared to observe from afar what was happening. One of the stories says, "There were also women looking on from a distance; among them were Mary Magdalene and Mary, the mother of James and of Joses, and Salome. These used to follow him and provided for him when he was in Galilee; and there were many other women who had come up with him to Jerusalem" (Mk. 15: 40-41). As you can see, it isn't until the end of Jesus' ministry that we find stories that tell us that women were a part of the movement. I know of only one story early in Jesus' ministry (long before our Lord Jesus was crucified) that specifically mentions that women accompanied him. In the story at the empty tomb, when the women were frightened at finding it empty because Jesus' body was gone, two angels comfort them saying, "Remember how he told you, when he was still in Galilee..." (Lk. 24:6).

These passages tell us that the movement of Jesus the Christ always included women disciples, apostles, and missionaries. But since the vocabulary of the accounts hides this fact, many people assume that at the beginning the movement was made up only of men. In closing then, I will tell you some of what we in the community here in Philippi know about women disciples and teachers, myself among them.

Note

1. See Carla Ricci, *Mary Magdalene and Many Others: Women Who Followed Jesus* (Minneapolis: Fortress Press, 1994), pp. 19-28.

Chapter 7

Mary Magdalene–Apostle and Friend of Jesus

(Mark 7: 24-30; Matthew 15: 21-28)

Mary Magdalene: the Most Frequently Mentioned Disciple

All of us here talk a lot about Mary Magdalene. She was the most important woman disciple in the movement of Jesus.[1] Perhaps even more significantly than Peter, she provided leadership to start up the movement again after it seemed to have failed after the death of Jesus. Jesus' love for her was very special; it even seems that the disciples were somewhat jealous of her.[2] One of the most outstanding factors that places her front and center is that she witnessed the resurrection of Jesus. In fact all the stories mention her name first in the list of witnesses (Mk. 16: 1-11; Mt. 28: 1; Lk. 24: 10; Jn. 20: 11-18). Jesus appeared to her first before appearing to any other disciple. I know it isn't good or worthy of our movement to create rivalries for "first place" as is common in our Greco-Roman culture, for Jesus was against this (Mk. 10: 35-45). But because Mary Magdalene was marginalized simply for being a woman, I feel it's important to remind you of her position. As I mentioned before, even Paul, my teacher, forgot to mention her in his list of our Lord's appearances (1 Cor. 15: 5-8).

Mary was from Magdala, a town near the shore of the Sea of Galilee. There is a lot of commercial activity in that region where the fishing industry is very important. I hope to visit that region some day to remember Mary Magdalene. It is probable that she left her home when she joined the movement of Jesus, since she is identified as the "Magdalene," in other words, from Magdala.

The stories reveal that Jesus had healed her before she joined the movement. They say that Jesus had cast 7 demons from her (Mk. 16: 9; Lk 8: 2). The number 7 in the Jewish culture always means fullness, which indicates that she had been quite overcome by her sickness. She had lost her dignity and sense of belonging as a result of the demons. She needed to "return to herself."[3] Based on other stories of the demon-possessed people that Jesus healed, I can imagine her sad life and worn body. I'm sure she was ostracized by those around her. Her healing experience must have been so important in her life that she decided to follow Jesus and travel with him through all the towns and villages where the movement took hold. I can imagine that walking with Jesus and seeing the life that other demon-possessed people led, and the changes in their lives when Jesus healed them, would have been a constant, powerful reminder of her own life. Perhaps this led to her steadfast following of Jesus; she truly understood and embodied what the Kingdom of God meant for the lives of these people. How very different from what the other disciples experienced! True, they observed the healings, but they had not experienced them in their own lives.

There is a story of another woman who was known in the city as a sinner (Lk. 7: 6-50). She was the one who kissed Jesus' feet and washed them with her tears, dried them with her hair and perfumed them. Some people think that this woman was Mary Magdalene, but she wasn't. That was another woman who loved Jesus and was welcomed by him in spite of her reputation as a sinner. And yet I don't think there is anything wrong with confusing Mary Magdalene with a prostitute, for many think she was the woman who was forgiven.[4] It only shows that Jesus respected all persons and had no problem welcoming into his movement women who had been prostitutes. The serious problem I, Lydia, see is that this confusion makes us forget the most important thing about Mary Magdalene: her apostleship. To many of us she holds equal status with Peter and Paul. Because of this omission, we women run the risk of being marginalized in the movement, for there are those with strong voices who claim that the apostleship was and is only for men. This Mary Magdalene could be remembered only as the repentant and forgiven sinner. But the stories about the resurrection and Mary's role cannot be silenced because they appear several times.

The Courage of Mary Magdalene

Mary Magdalene was very brave. She appeared to have been a leader among the women because she was almost always with a group of women and was the spokesperson. When Jesus was crucified, she and other women dared to leave the hiding place (Jn. 20: 9) of all the disciples to see what they could do for Jesus. They took the risk. All of us who live in provinces that are under Roman domination, or in Roman colonies, know the grave danger that friends and family of crucified persons face.[5] They aren't allowed to be close by and are forbidden to cry or mourn publicly. Sometimes, if they dare to cry, they are crucified as well. Those who are crucified must not be covered or hidden from sight so they can serve as a lesson to others. Their bodies are not buried, but left for animals to scavenge. This is part of the shame that the crucified must suffer and why they are closely guarded so that family and friends don't steal their bodies and give them proper burial. The Roman guards don't even show respect for children or mothers.[6] Crucifixion is greatly abused in our time.[7]

In spite of this, Mary Magdalene, along with some other women, dared to witness Jesus' painful death. They watched everything from a distance: how he was crucified and where he was buried. Jesus was buried thanks to an important man, Joseph of Arimathea who asked Pilate, the Roman procurator, for permission to bury him (Mk. 15: 42-47; Lk. 23: 50-56; Jn. 19: 38-42).

Although the story is told in different ways, all of them tell how Mary Magdalene[8] and the other women went very early after the Sabbath to the tomb where they had seen Jesus buried. They wanted to do the customary rite of honor for the dead by anointing his body with perfume.[9]

These women knew that they had to be very cautious in going to the tomb; they must have been terrified, knowing the political danger of visiting or being present at the tomb of a person who had been crucified. But Mary Magdalene, a decisive woman, was willing to go and was accompanied by other women. Different versions of the story give different names for the women who watched the crucifixion from afar and went to the tomb. Among them were: first,

Mary Magdalene, then Mary, the mother of James, and Mary, the mother of Joses and Salome.[10]

Neither the women nor the rest of the disciples knew that Jesus had arisen from the dead, so their intent was to honor the body of their dead leader. Along the way they talked about the difficulties. "Who would move the stone?" they asked themselves. I understand a tomb was closed with a heavy stone that required a lever to move it. But when the women arrived, the stone had been removed. They didn't find the body. Can you imagine their fright at this discovery? In the midst of their fear they experienced God through a messenger, God's angel (Mk. 16: 5; Mt. 28: 2) or two angels, as some say (Lk. 24: 4). In addition to Moses, the patriarchs and prophets, several women have experienced God this way, that is, in an epiphany;* among them were Hagar, the Egyptian slave, and Mary, the mother of Jesus. These few women of the movement of Jesus, those who dared to go to the tomb, also experienced an epiphany, while the rest of the disciples, both men and women, hid for fear of repression. This daring deed must be told. Because there are no men in the story, however, it tends to be forgotten or considered of little importance. Instead, the resurrection epiphany story usually starts in the upper room where the men are finally present (Lk. 24: 30-34).

Women: the First Witnesses to and Preachers about the Resurrection

Not only were these women, led by Mary Magdalene, the first persons to witness the resurrection, they also received the commission to communicate the good news to the rest of the disciples. They were to tell them that Jesus would be going to Galilee and would see them there again (Mk. 16: 5-7; Mt. 28: 1-8; Lk. 24: 1-10). There is even a story that states that, when they were getting ready to tell the disciples the good news, Jesus himself appeared (Mt. 28: 9). I dearly love Paul of Tarsus, but we need to remind him of this fact as well. Another story describes the women as so scared they didn't say anything to anyone (Mk. 16: 8). This may have been true for a moment—and to be expected—considering the situation they were in. Obviously they did tell it later because we have the news and know they were witnesses to it. If the women had kept silent, everyone would have thought that the movement had failed. And if it had, I, Lydia, wouldn't be telling you this today.

Mary Magdalene: the Apostle Who Was Close to Jesus

One of the stories mentions only Mary Magdalene at the tomb (Jn. 20). She arrived at dawn while it was still dark and found the stone removed. She was frightened, thinking that the body of Jesus had been stolen, and ran to tell Peter and John.[11] This account tells us that Mary Magdalene was very sad; she missed Jesus and suffered because of his absence. But when she was outside the tomb, God was manifested (an epiphany) through two angels that asked her why she was crying. She answered that it was because someone had stolen the body of Jesus (Jn. 20: 13). She cried, as do those who have had friends or family members who have been tortured and assassinated, and whose bodies have disappeared.[12]

When Jesus appeared to her, she thought it was the person in charge of the garden and that he might know where the body was. She asked him about the body because she wanted to get it back and take it with her (Jn. 20: 15). But that was impossible. I, Lydia, believe that Mary had to understand that the leader of the movement now had a resurrected body. His Spirit would be present not only among his small group of followers in Galilee, but would be poured out on many others who didn't know him, such as my community here in Philippi, in all of Macedonia, and the other provinces of the Empire. Jesus made this known to her.

Every time I hear the dialogue between Jesus and Mary Magdalene it makes me want to cry; it is a very emotional moment. He called her by name, like the good shepherd who calls his sheep; he said to her, "Mary!" She immediately recognized the sound of his voice, for she had followed him and his group for quite some time. She answered immediately, "Rabbouni!" like the disciple who identifies his or her master, the sheep that knows its shepherd. Such was her love for him that she wanted to hold on to him and not let go. The story doesn't tell us if she embraced him or threw herself at his feet like the women in the other story (Mt. 28: 9). What they do tell us is that Jesus said to her, "Do not hold on to me."[13] No one can have Jesus all to themselves. No matter how much we love him he is no one's private property for he belongs to all the communities.

In person, Jesus gave her the message she needed to take to the other disciples. He revealed to her the mystery of the resurrection and the divine solidarity that takes place when God the Father of Jesus Christ becomes the Father of us all. For I believe that in the moment God becomes our Father, and all of us become children of God, not Jesus only: "'my Father and your Father, my God and your God'" (Jn. 20: 17).

I, Lydia, consider Mary Magdalene to have been a true apostle. She had all the necessary qualifications that are established by the church today for someone to be called an apostle. She followed and was a part of the movement of Jesus in Galilee, and witnessed his death and resurrection. I see, however, that she is being excluded. Could it be that she went to Galilee with other women and established a community there that we don't know about and that was considered to be of little importance by the Christian community in Jerusalem?[14] Perhaps. What I know is that she has been excluded from the organized community in Jerusalem. I am afraid that as time goes by, the values that were established at the beginning of the movement in Galilee are gradually being eroded. If this happens, our communities will lose the spirit of the movement and the marginalization of women will increase little by little.[15]

As a leader in the movement, I intend always to remember Mary Magdalene as a disciple and teacher, and I encourage you to do the same!

Notes

1. See Carla Ricci, *Mary Magdalene and Many Others* (Minneapolis: Fortress Press, 1994), pp. 139ff. Also see Elisabeth Moltmann-Wandel, *The Women Around Jesus* (New York: The Crossroad Publishing Co., 1992), pp. 68ff.

2. This is obvious in apocryphal texts such as the "Gospel of Philip," 55, and in the "Gospel of Thomas," 114. These appear in James M. Robinson, *The Nag Hammadi Library in English* (New York: Harper & Row, 1977), pp. 133-134 and 130.

3. "return to self," Carla Ricci, *Mary Magdalene and Many Others*, p. 139.

4. The story doesn't say anything about the type of sin she was known for. According to Sharon Ringe, a sinner could be called a "sinner" if she was known

to be a liar, thief, cheater or dishonest. The only thing that indicates she is a prostitute is the fact that she let her hair loose–considered to be immoral in a woman–and that she had perfumes that she could have used with her clients. *Luke* (Louisville: Westminster John Knox Press, 1995), p. 108.

5. This is because subversives and slaves were punished by crucifixion.

6. Concerning the danger and severity of the soldiers with the family members, see Luise Schottroff, *Mulheres no Novo Testamento. Exegese numa Perspectiva Feminista* (São Paulo: Paulinas, 1995), pp. 44-48; Ivoni Richter Reimer, "Recordar, transmitir, actuar. Mujeres en los comienzos del cristianismo" in *Revista de Investigación Bíblica Latinoamericana* (RIBLA), no. 22 (1996), p. 50.

7. At various instances during this time, the Romans held mass, indiscriminate crucifixions. See Neil Elliott, *Liberating Paul: The Justice of God and the Politics of the Apostle* (Maryknoll, New York: Orbis Books, 1994), p. 94.

8. Luke talks about the women who followed from Galilee, without giving their names, but in 24: 10 he names three who were supposed to have been there. John mentions only Mary Magdalene.

9. See Luise Schottroff, *Mulheres no Novo Testamento*, pp. 44-48.

10. Again, only John mentions Mary Magdalene. Luke doesn't give all the names of the women at the tomb. But in 24: 10 he tells who the women were who gave the message of the resurrection upon returning from the tomb: "Now it was Mary Magdalene, Joanna, Mary the mother of James, and the other women with them...."

11. The assumption is that the disciple whom the Lord loved was John. The writer of the Gospel of John wants Peter and John also to be witnesses to the resurrection (20: 1-10), although the epiphany—appearance of Jesus—was experienced only by Mary Magdalene (20: 11-18). During the time in which the Gospels were written, the supremacy of Peter, James, and John had been well established. The Synoptic Gospels, however, describe only the women. Because their presence was so evident, the authors could not eliminate them.

12. It was common in the late 20th century to hear of the "disappearance" of persons in Latin America (and other continents) who were never accounted for.

13. The Greek verb in the present imperative implies that the contact is being carried out uninterruptedly. Therefore it cannot be translated "touch me not" (as in the King James Version), but rather "stop touching me" or "let go of me." J. Mateos and J. Barreto, *El evangelio de Juan* (Madrid: Cristiandad, 1982), p. 852.

14. See Suzanne Tunc, *También las mujeres seguían a Jesús* (Santander: Sal Terrae, 1999), p. 91. Another possible explanation for Mary Magdalene's marginalization by tradition is that this woman was admired by heretical groups such as the Gnostics. See also Elisa Esteves, "La mujer en la tradición del discípulo amado," in *Revista de Interpretación Bíblica Latinoamericana* (RIBLA), no.17 (1994). In the apocryphal books we observe a constant rivalry between Peter and Mary Magdalene, reflecting the discussion between the communities that wanted to establish formal parameters for institutionalization. Thus the movement of Jesus as such ceased to exist and became an institution.

15. This is what happened later on, as observed in the post-Pauline and pastoral writings such as Eph. 3: 8, Col. 1: 23, 1 Tim. 2: 8-11.

Chapter 8

The Woman Who Was a Missionary from Samaria

(John 4: 5-42)

I am going to tell you the story of a Samaritan woman. In the community here we all consider her to be the first woman to share the good news of Jesus in her region. Besides this, there are three other aspects to this story of Jesus' encounter with this woman that we need to consider as well. First, we must take into account the fact that Samaria and Judea are two regions in permanent conflict due to their cultural and religious differences. Second, Jesus dared to speak with a woman from Samaria who was also of dubious reputation (she had had five husbands and the man she was living with was not her husband). Third, the message of Jesus transcended all cultural differences and discrimination, whether ethnic, sexist or any other kind.

I have already mentioned that one of the main characteristics of the movement of Jesus was that in the vison of the Kingdom of God, there is no discrimination. Everyone is treated as brothers and sisters and they serve each other mutually. Today, after Jesus' death and resurrection, I see this value present in the communities, although there are those who tend to forget it. Paul of Tarsus reminds us of it when we are baptized saying, that in Christ, the Messiah, "there is no longer Jew or Greek, there is no longer slave or free, there is no longer male and female, for all of you are one in Christ Jesus" (Gal. 3:28).[1] How I would love for the communities always to remember this! It is a teaching that we learn from the very life of Jesus of Nazareth. We have seen it in the many stories I have told you and here, in the story of the Samaritan woman, we will see it again.

On the Margin of Mutual Hate

Samaria is a region located between Galilee to the north and Judea to the south. People say that when the Jews from Galilee have to go to Jerusalem for feasts or other matters, they try to avoid Samaria by going around it, generally by way of the Jordan River. The conflicts between Samaritans and Jews date back several centuries. The inhabitants of Samaria derive from two groups. One group is made up of those who remained when Assyria conquered Samaria and took the upper class Samaritans as captives. The other group is from Babylon and Median. They are immigrants who came from other cultures and regions as a result of the forced evictions and colonizations of the Assyrians. In time the diverse population and its beliefs mixed. The Jews, in keeping with their purity system that we have referred to in other stories, considered Samaritans to be impure because of their mixed blood.

But that isn't all. The Samaritans refused to accept the Temple of Jerusalem as their temple and many years ago built their own altar on Mt. Gerizim to worship God. Years later, when the Jews returned from exile in Babylon and started to rebuild Jerusalem, the Samaritans opposed it. Their mutual hate can be observed in several incidents. John Hyrcanus, a Jewish high priest, set fire to the Samaritan temple of Gerizim (128 B.C.E.). Before that, the Samaritans had helped the kings of Syria in the wars against the Jews. It is told that around Jesus' birth (4 B.C.E.), some Samaritans profaned the Temple in Jerusalem during the Passover, leaving human bones in the atriums. After that they were prohibited from entering the Temple.[2]

I understand that there are religious differences between Samaritans and Jews. For example, the Samaritans accept only the first five books of Moses, and not the books of the Prophets or the Wisdom Literature, as Holy Scripture. The Messiah they anticipated was not the same one the Jews expected. The Jews were looking for a nationalistic Messiah, a descendant of David, while the Samaritans expected a Messiah like Moses, and so were waiting for the Toheb, or master of the law.[3]

In spite of all this, or perhaps because of it, Jesus decided to pass through Samaria.[4] The story tells us that Jesus arrived in Sychar,[5] a city in Samaria, where he felt tired and sat down near a source of water called Jacob's Well. He had probably walked far; peasants like Jesus were used to walking long distances. It was the sixth hour (midday), when the sun is strongest and thirst from the intense heat is greatest. The disciples had gone to the city to buy food. A woman from the region approached the well to draw water. It seems odd to me (and probably Jesus) that the woman would draw water at this time of day; generally it is done at dawn or sunset. The woman must have been startled to see a Jew sitting there! The Samaritans expected nothing more than rejection from the Jews. They knew that to call someone a "Samaritan" was a grave insult.[6] The woman's astonishment must have been even greater when Jesus asked her, "Give me a drink" (Jn. 4:7). Her astonishment would explain why she didn't respond with the customary expression of hospitality and draw water for him. Instead she said: "How is it that you, a Jew, ask a drink of me, a woman of Samaria?" She knew that the Jews considered themselves to be superior, the way men feel superior to women. There was a racist saying at that time that one could never count on the ritual purity of Samaritan women because they menstruated from the time they were in the crib.[7] But I believe that this woman by her question demonstrated neither submission nor belief in what was said about the Samaritans. Perhaps she answered boldly, and perhaps somewhat sarcastically: "So now you humble yourself, because you are thirsty?"

The rules of social behavior of that time did not look favorably upon men conversing with women. It was said by the teachers, "Don't detain yourself for a long while to speak with a woman."[8] The disciples, upon their return from the city, were surprised at seeing Jesus talking with the woman. However, they knew that their leader sometimes ignored social norms in his preaching, teaching, healing, and other actions, and so didn't dare question him (see Jn. 4: 27).

When the woman asked Jesus why *he*, a Jew, was asking *her* for water, Jesus took advantage of the situation to speak of deeper things. He disregarded the enmity between the two peoples and the fact that he was speaking with a woman. Once again, we see how the movement of Jesus was concerned with new relationships between human beings in which there is not hate but rather mutual solidarity, and where no culture or belief is to be superior to another. That is why he went straight to the point and little by little revealed to her his identity as the Messiah.

A Theological Dialogue by the Well

Jesus revealed himself to the Samaritan woman as "living water" (Jn. 4: 10), a kind of water that never runs out and that quenches thirst forever. For those who drink it, the water becomes a spring flowing to give eternal life (Jn. 4: 13, 14). I believe that the water is the Spirit of God, and with that Spirit all enmity and discrimination cease. We would never need to return to the well of Jacob, which symbolizes the law, because whoever drinks from *that* well becomes thirsty again and must constantly return to it.

At first the woman didn't understand everything Jesus was saying. Neither did the disciples understand when later, in that same place, Jesus spoke to them about another type of food (4: 33, 34). Jesus wanted his disciples and followers to understand from the beginning a new kind of human relationship and life together in which their sustenance came from fulfilling the will of God (Jn. 4: 34).

For a moment, the dialogue between Jesus and the woman touched upon her private life. Jesus asked her to bring her husband; the woman answered that she had none. At that point Jesus described her life to her: "You have had five husbands and the one you have now is not your husband" (Jn. 4: 16-18). I, Lydia, have learned that the law allowed two marriages, and three as the limit, but she had been married four times and lived with a man who was not her husband. Her sexual life was not praiseworthy in the eyes of her society. The story tells us nothing about the feelings of this woman towards the Jewish stranger who seemed to know her past life. It only tells us that it surprised and impressed her to have someone describe her life.

I have heard some interpret the story symbolically, stating that there is a play on the word "ba'al" that means Lord. Ba'al is the God of the Canaanites, but can also mean husband. If that were so, Jesus would have been referring to the idolatry of the Samaritans. The five husbands represented the five altars to the gods which the history of Israel mentions (2 Kings 17: 24-41).[9] The current "husband," then, would be Yahweh, the God of Israel who, according to the Jews, does not belong completely to the Samaritans.

But I think the Samaritan woman's situation could have been real. That is, for a variety of reasons—through divorce or death—she could have had five husbands, and a current companion to whom she was not married. She would have been pushed to the edges of society for her moral behavior. It would not have been unusual for Jesus to initiate with this woman the dialogue that would lead to the conversion of many in Samaria. This was Jesus' favorite way of doing things. The woman began to believe Jesus was a prophet, because he told her facts about herself without having known her.[10]

Jesus continued to dialogue with the woman about the deep things of God, the different places of worship, the way to worship, salvation, and the Messiah for whom they were waiting. I particularly like this. Too often men think that we women lack the ability to carry out a deep dialogue about God. But this story reveals how Jesus spoke to the woman as if she were an expert in the law to whom he wanted to show another way. She had her doubts due to her own ingrained tradition, and she asked questions. Little by little Jesus introduced her to the newness of life that he offered.

They discussed the conflict between Jews and Samaritans. She said that the Jews worship in Jerusalem where they say God must be worshiped, but as a Samaritan she knew the Samaritans worshiped on the sacred mountain of Gerizim. Then Jesus showed her that for those who worship in Spirit and in truth, it is not important where it is done—whether at the Temple in Jerusalem or in Samaria. I see that Jesus, as a Jew, was critical of Judaism as well as of all cultures and belief systems that consider themselves to be the only true one. True worshipers are those who worship God in Spirit and in truth, anywhere in the world. For me, God is Spirit and graces us with God's spirit so that all people can experience a new birth.[11]

The Samaritan Woman Takes the Good News to Her Neighbors

Jesus presented himself to the Samaritan woman as the Messiah (Jn. 4: 26), a Messiah who was different from the one whom the Jews or Samaritans awaited. I believe that Jesus-Messiah transcended the barriers of nationality that led to discrimination and gave new meaning to the understanding of the law. Jesus offered himself as a gift of God, as living water, grace and freedom that are present in the new life in Christ. Paul of Tarsus has shown us this as well.

It is curious to me, Lydia, that Jesus had no misgivings about presenting himself to a woman as the Messiah, while avoiding use of this title with the Jews. Perhaps he felt able to announce this to the Samaritan woman because Samaritans didn't have the concept of a monarch-messiah, a descendant of David, who would rule with power over all of Israel. In any case, it is significant for me as a woman that Jesus revealed himself in this way to a woman who, besides being a Samaritan, was looked upon unfavorably for her moral conduct. As Jesus revealed his identity to her, the disciples returned and were surprised to find him talking with a woman, a Samaritan. They would have been even more surprised had they known what the two were discussing! But Jesus soon began another conversation about God with his disciples (Jn. 4: 31-38).

The woman then left her water jar and returned quickly to the city. The joy and the surprise this Jewish man from Galilee had given her were so great that she couldn't hold back the desire to share it with others. I think she began to grow in feelings of self-worth and dignity as she experienced that she had been taken seriously, as all women should be respected and taken seriously. When she arrived in the city, she spoke to her neighbors about her experience with this man named Jesus, who called himself Messiah and had told her her story without knowing her. Surely this had an impact on the people of her country. For the story tells us that "many Samaritans from that city believed in him because of the woman's testimony" (Jn. 4: 39). She was the first evangelist to tell the Good News in Samaria.

I ask myself how it was possible that a woman of such reputation was believed. Could it be that she was so transformed by her experience with Jesus that it had a profound and convincing impact on the people of that place? Perhaps her eloquent words and transformed presence were significant signs to those who knew her.

She managed to get the Samaritans of her city to go see Jesus and speak with him so that they could experience firsthand the encounter that she had had. The story concludes by telling us that Jesus stayed with them two days. Others also had the life-changing encounter that invites people to be born again and to belong to the communities of the movement of Jesus. Because the woman at Jacob's Well dared to respond to Jesus' comments and unorthodox behavior, her life was forever changed. She, in turn, participated in the transformation of other lives through her courageous behavior.

I, Lydia, hope that this Spirit of Jesus will touch many people. Both Jesus and the Samaritan woman defied the social rules of their cultures and challenged the prejudices and disputes between Jew and Samaritan, men and women. As a resident of Greco-Roman society, I know that it is very difficult to live in such equality in a stratified and patriarchal society. I am a witness to the difficulties and conflicts we face when we try to live this way.

Notes

1. This is a pre-Pauline baptismal formula.

2. J. Mateos and J. Barretos, *El evangelio de Juan* (Madrid: Cristiandad, 1982), p. 228.

3. Raymond Brown, *The Gospel According to John (I-XII)* (New York: Doubleday & Co., Inc. 1966), p. 374.

4. He could have detoured around Samaria through Transjordan, but Jesus wanted to go through Samaria; he was not forced to do so.

5. It is difficult to place this city. Some think it refers to Shechem (Brown, *The Gospel According to John*, p. 371); others, to the "Askar" of current times (José Blank, *O Evangelho Segundo João* [Petrópolis: Vozes,1990], p. 299). Askar has a well about half a mile from the city.

6. Henri van den Bussche, *El evangelio según San Juan* (Madrid: Studium, 1972), p. 226.

7. Raymond Brown, *The Gospel According to John*, p. 179.

8. Jose ben Yohanan (150 A.D.) mentioned in Wikenhauser, *El evangelio según San Juan* (Barcelona: Herder, 1967), p. 170.

9. Most commentaries mention this possibility.

10. The Samaritans' understanding of a prophet was different from the Jews'. The Samaritans had Deuteronomy 18: 15-22 in mind.

11. Raymond Brown, *The Gospel According to John*, p. 179. According to Brown, the fact that God is a Spirit does not refer to God's essence, but rather to God's relationship with human beings.

Chapter 9

Priscilla and Lydia– Two Working Women, Leaders of Christian Communities

(Acts 16: 11-15, 40; 18: 1-4, 18-19, 24-28; Romans 16: 3)

I'm not going to tell you any more stories. The stories I have shared are enough evidence of the presence of courageous women in the movement of Jesus, before and after his death, both in and out of Palestine. I'm sure that there were many more women; I have heard of some and many are stories that have never been told. In these last pages I want to give you my testimony and that of Priscilla, a great woman, who was partner of Aquila. She and I are very much alike, and there are many more like us. I have heard more about her from Paul, because he mentions her frequently. In fact, thanks to Paul, I know about the many women leaders outside of Philippi. But our movement is growing and so there are many others whom I don't know because they are not involved in Paul's ministry.[1]

Lydia: Leader and Business Woman

I still remember with satisfaction the day I was introduced to the movement of Jesus, the Christ,[2] and became a part of it. It was through the Apostle Paul. I have always been a very active participant in religious activities. I continue to go to a place of prayer outside of the city (Acts 16: 13) that we call *proseuche*. It is a place set aside for the Sabbath services where the Jews have their liturgies. These places of worship are almost always outside the city gates near a river. Because some religions might at any time come into conflict with Roman customs, practitioners are obligated to build a meeting place outside the city.[3] Such is the case here in Philippi.

One day I was at this place of prayer with some other women when Paul and Silas arrived and began to speak to us. Paul spoke wonderful things about Jesus. His invitation to become children of God in a "new creation" made an impact on me. As you know, I am a Gentile but have converted to Judaism. I decided then to give my allegiance also to the Jew, Jesus, the Christ, and so I became a member of his movement. I was baptized with all those of my household (Acts 16: 14-15). I was the leader of the group of women who were at the place of prayer, and they followed my example.

My house became a meeting place for the community of Jesus, the Christ. It was the first and continues to grow. In my house-church, as in all the others, we try to live in communion among brothers and sisters. As owner of the house, I am at the head of the house-church. Many times I lead the meetings and administer the working of the group. I try to help economically because the majority of our members earn less income than I do.

As head of the community, I am also responsible for protecting our members as well as visitors from other places.[4] Sometimes situations of conflict become critical for member of our community, and it is my responsibility to provide protection for political prisoners. For example, Paul and Silas were imprisoned for the conflict that arose between them and the owners of a slave girl who earned a lot of money for the oracles she pronounced. Paul freed her of the spirit of divination and her masters, furious, took Paul and Silas to court and accused them of being Jewish troublemakers who spoke of customs that the Romans could not accept or practice. The city magistrates ordered the missionaries to be stripped and flogged, then jailed in the deepest dungeon, with their feet set in the stocks (Acts 16: 16-24). After they were set free, they came to my house. I know it is dangerous for my family, our community and me, but I am pleased to be able to receive them. I believe that our community must put into practice the teachings of Jesus of Nazareth, who was crucified and died for proclaiming the Kingdom of God.

The missionaries like Paul and Silas know the risk we run when we welcome them. Sometimes they do not want to put us in danger. One time I had to prevail[5] upon them to stay in my house (Acts 16: 15). I know that the itinerant Jewish preachers are often in danger because they speak of things that threaten the economic interests of some (see Acts 16: 16-24; 19: 23-40). My duty is to offer them hospitality and protection from political persecution. I have decided to take the risk because I am a follower of Jesus.[6] The same is true for the entire community.

The responsibility and work involved in leading the community is great, but that isn't all I do. As you know I sell purple cloth, a job that has me traveling constantly, especially to Thyatira, where I was born and where I get the purple cloth. It is abundant there and many kinds can be found at good prices. Many people think I am rich because I sell this purple cloth[7] and that this makes things easier for me. Well, let me clarify that I don't sell the cloth colored with the purple dye that comes from a mollusk found only in certain coastal regions. That is a luxury article, as I explained before, and only the very wealthy can buy it. The administration of the Empire has had a monopoly on it for quite some time. The cloth I sell is colored from another dye that comes from a plant. I use it because it's much cheaper and even slaves use it to dye some of their cloths. In addition, there are several taxes that I have to pay, including customs taxes and the one for being a foreigner. It adds up to a lot.

But I am not poor, like some of the women in the stories I've told you. I am a "freedwoman" and, like other freedwomen and slaves of the same trade, I make a living by working hard. I have my trade, am respected for it, and belong to an association with others who have the same trade.[8] This trade of dyeing and selling purple cloth is generally carried out by a group of freedwomen and slaves. Several of my friends who worship in the *proseuche* or place of prayer do the same kind of work I do.

But the truth is that in spite of the work, or perhaps because of my work in the community of believers and in commerce, I feel satisfied as a woman. I have never felt in our Greco-Roman society the profound equality between men and women that we seek to live out in the faith community. We mutually respect and help each other–men and women, masters and slaves, and those of different cultures. We don't follow a hierarchic leadership style in the house-church. Many times I lead the services because I am the owner of the house. But because I travel a lot, others lead as well. Of course, we have problems. Living together with different kinds of people is not easy. This way of living is new to us. Some have had a hard time getting used to the leadership of women, for example. And yet for us as women, the external pressure we feel from the stereotypes of the roles we are expected to fulfill is very strong. But we continue to move forward, discussing, fighting, reconciling and seeking to be faithful to God in prayer and in solidarity with each other.

I am not unique as a leader of a community who makes her living by a trade. Many leaders and missionaries of the communities practice a profession or trade. Like Paul of Tarsus, Priscilla is a tentmaker as is her partner Aquila. Through our work as artisans or merchants, we gain opportunities for presenting the Good News of Jesus the Messiah because we have lots of contact with all kinds of people. This helps us to share the Gospel in a way that is pertinent.

Priscilla: Leader, Teacher and Artisan

As I look at Priscilla's life, I see we are very much alike but also very different. We share in common that we are both leaders and workers with all that that implies. But our differences point out how we as Christian women move about the provinces of the Empire, outside of Palestine.

Priscilla is a Jew from Pontus in Asia Minor. She married another Jew, Aquila. As tentmakers (Acts 18: 3) and missionaries, they travel quite a bit. They have lived in many different places, sometimes the result of political or economic circumstances and sometimes because of their missonary activities. At one point in their lives, they lived in Rome but were expelled, together with other converted Jews, and went to Corinth. It was there that they met Paul and after a while traveled with him to Ephesus and then returned to Rome. In Corinth, Ephesus, and Rome the house of Priscilla and Aquila has been one of the house-churches where believers have come together.

Priscilla is very well-known among us. Her name usually appears first when both she and Aquila are spoken of. In our culture this means that in her missionary work, education, and perhaps even in business her participation is significant with respect to that of her husband. Sometimes, although rarely, Aquila's name shows up first (Acts 18: 2 and 1 Cor. 16: 19), which indicates that both were active in ministry. Priscilla also stands out for her authority in teaching. She and Aquila decided to give Apollos, the famous and eloquent leader from Alexandria, a more detailed explanation concerning the movement of Jesus, the Christ (Acts 18: 26). What surprised me was that Apollos allowed himself to be taught by a couple in which the woman was more important than the man. This shows us two things: first, the authority and ability of Priscilla and Aquila with respect to the message; and second, the willingness on behalf of eloquent male leaders to recognize the ability and equality of women within the movement in direct contrast to the discriminatory practices of the patriarchal society.

Generally those who follow the trade of tent-making are slaves and freedpersons. Paul, Priscilla and Aquila are neither and, as is the custom, they join to work together. Even though they are not slaves or freedpersons, they suffer the same stigma and are looked upon as though they were because of their profession. It is hard work, perhaps more difficult than mine. Paul talks about having to work day and night to support himself. (2 Thess. 3: 8).

I was converted thanks to Paul, but Priscilla and Aquila had been converted before the apostle. When Paul came to Corinth for the first time, they were already there, having just been exiled from Rome by the decree of Claudius (Acts 18: 2). It seems that the Romans only deported converted Jews; the decree states that they were to be deported because of one called Christ.[9] Paul came into contact with them in Corinth and went to live at their house. There the three of them worked together making tents and preaching the Good News of the Gospel. Paul refers to Priscilla as a coworker on the same level as he. However, she and Aquila are independent and not under Paul's authority.[10]

I'm not sure exactly how their business went, but Corinth is a good city in which to prosper. There is very active commercial traffic and thus great diversity among its people. Due to its geographic position, there is much political and military activity. To reach the eastern part of the Empire from Italy (Italia), and vice versa, it is necessary to cross the Isthmus of Corinth.[11] Corinth is a city that was repopulated with Roman colonists and surely there are many war veterans, as there are here in Philippi. Priscilla and

Aquila, together with Paul, remained for quite some time in that city, probably creating several house-church communities like their own. The houses in Greco-Roman cities are not large, in fact are quite small which means that generally several small house-groups meet. Sometimes we all get together for a special event in the larger home of one of the wealthier families. But the most we can accommodate is some 40 or 50 people, perhaps 9 or 10 in the *triclinius* (dining room) with the rest standing in the *atrium*, if the owner of the house doesn't have any more furniture.[12]

Priscilla must have been witness to some of the conflicts among the people of Corinth. Paul tells the brothers and sisters here that one time in Corinth the Jews who didn't like him pressed accusations before Gallio, proconsul of Achaia, charging Paul with contradicting the law. Since Gallio didn't pay much attention to them, a fight broke out right there outside the courts! Sosthenes, the chief rabbi of the synagogue, was caught by surprise and beaten up (Acts 18: 12-17).[13]

Such is our life in this society. As missionaries and leaders we are witnesses to these conflicts. Perhaps Priscilla was a witness to other serious conflicts that took place in Ephesus, when the three of them–Priscilla, Aquila, and Paul–went there and the couple separated from Paul. He stayed a while, left and then returned to stay for a longer period. Priscilla and Aquila could have been at Ephesus when Paul had the problem with the makers of the statue of Artemis, the most important goddess in the region (Acts 19: 23-41). But the problem arose because the economic interests of the statue-makers had been affected. They earned a lot of money making the silver statues and feared that their business would fail as a result of Paul's preaching. Paul was saved from danger that time because his friends didn't allow him to go near the theater (Acts 19: 30-31) where many of the furious statue-makers gathered to discuss the problem. He was forced to leave the city.

Paul was very grateful to Priscilla and Aquila, because when this tumult happened in Ephesus, and when he was in jail, the couple risked their lives to save him, and other members of the community. Paul would never forget that courageous expression of solidarity (Rom. 16: 3).

I, Lydia, a worker and teacher like Priscilla, can say that up until now we do not know of any group that organizes itself in a way that provides for such equality in its relationships, or solidarity and commitment as that of our house-churches. It is true that some clubs, guilds or associations admit slaves and women as equals, but the patron of the association always expects to receive due honor.[14] It is not like that among us. Jesus taught us that the greatest must serve the least. As women we feel welcome and respected. There are many of us because we have found in the communities of believers a place of freedom and resistance against the social and religious marginalization of women.

Notes

1. Schüssler Fiorenza affirms that the women who acted independently of Paul were not registered in history. We know more from Paul's letters. Paul was the one who spoke the most about women. *In Memory of Her: A Feminist Theological Reconstruction of Christian Origins* (New York: The Crossroad Publishing Co., 1994), p. 184.

2. Lydia must now add the term "Christ" when speaking of the movement of Jesus, because it refers to Jesus after the resurrection, when the movement extends beyond Palestine.

3. I know of one by Ivoni Richter Reimer. I extracted some of the data from her analysis in *Vida de Mulheres na Sociedade e na Igreja* (São Paulo: Paulinas, 1995), pp. 60-79.

4. Schüssler Fiorenza, *In Memory of Her*, p. 181.

5. According to Ivoni Richter Reimer, the Greek term *parabiazestai* or "force" is used in the greater and extra-biblical literary, historical, and political contexts primarily to offer protection and shelter to someone who is suffering or will suffer persecution and threats. *Vida de Mulheres*, p. 77.

6. Luise Schottroff refers to the risk that Lydia takes when she offers hospitality to Paul and Silas. She has to persuade Paul by affirming even her fidelity to the Lord. *Lydia's Impatient Sisters: A Feminist Social History of Early Christianity* (Louisville: Westminster John Knox Press, 1995), p. 110.

7. Most scholars have held this opinion. Current research, however, places doubt upon it. See Ivoni Richter Reimer, *Vida de Mulheres*, p.73f.

8. Here we are referring to the associations (collegia) and private guilds that were common at that time, generally made up of people with similar trade or religious interests. Irene Foulkes, *Problemas pastorales en Corinto* (San José: DEI/SBL, 1996), p. 49f.

9. The decree is made in the year 49 C.E. (A.D.) and is noted by the historian Suetonius. Most scholars agree that "Cresto" was Christ. In the Latin of those times the letters e and i were often interchangeable.

10. See Schüssler Fiorenza, *In Memory of Her*, p. 178.

11. See Irene Foulkes, *Problemas pastorales*, p. 30.

12. Ibid., p. 306.

13. The text is not clear about who beat up Sosthenes. Justo González summarizes and explains three hypotheses: the Greeks, a mob from the city; the Jews angry with Sosthenes for letting himself be humiliated by Gallio; and the Jews who thought Sosthenes was inclined to favor the Christians. *Hechos: Comentario Bíblico Hispano* (Miami: Editorial Caribe, 1992), p. 262.

14. Schüssler Fiorenza, *In Memory of Her*, p. 181.

Conclusion

Let Women Not Be Silent in the Congregation

I, Elsa Tamez, a Mexican who resides in Costa Rica, have shared with you the beautiful stories of women through the voice of Lydia. But the stories and actual presence of women did not continue to be as significant in the following years. Toward the end of the first century, we observe a process that eliminates, little by little, the participation of women in the church. Women had achieved much in the movement of Jesus and in the early communities, especially those founded by Paul,[1] although not without conflict. However, the tensions and conflicts soon began to deepen as external Roman patriarchal social and cultural pressure worsened, and the institutionalization of the movement was deemed necessary. All this led to a gradual elimination or reduction of the rights that women had acquired in the movement of Jesus, the Christ. An obvious example was the treatment of Priscilla. Justo González writes:

> In the text (Greek), the name Priscilla appears before that of Aquila. By the II century the western text (Greek) inverted the order saying that Aquila and Priscilla were the ones who called Apollos aside....One of the ancient churches of Rome had been called, during the IV century, the "Church of Saint Prisca." Shortly afterward it was referred to as "of Prisca and Aquila" and by the VII century it was the church of "Saints Aquila and Prisca."[2]

What Happened?

Numerous studies prove the extensive participation of women in the early Christian church. There were many women like Lydia and Priscilla, both within and outside of Palestine. We know of Tabitha in Joppa; she is mentioned as a disciple of the movement of Jesus who was famous for her good works (Acts 9: 36-43). We know also of Mary, the mother of John Mark, who had a house-church in Jerusalem, because the text explicitly says that the believers were gathered there in prayer when Peter arrived after being set free from prison (Acts 12: 12). It is very probable that there were house-churches in Galilee with women leaders because after the death of Jesus, the women from Galilee who had followed him returned to their villages. They had come face to face with the resurrected Jesus and would have been eager to share the experience. Unfortunately, we don't know anything about these house-churches.

The list of greetings that appears in chapter 16 of Paul's letter to the Romans (57 C.E.) is a valuable historic document that confirms the participation of women in different ministries, many times at the same level as the Apostle Paul. A woman, Phoebe,[3] was responsible for taking the letter to Rome. Phoebe was a high-ranking person with prominent directive functions. Paul calls her "sister," "minister" and "protector." She is a *diakonos* or diaconal minister (a masculine Greek term that indicates official status here), a title that refers to the entire church of Cenchreae and not to a specific type of ministry. (The word does not appear in Acts 6, where it talks about the service of the tables.) The title *diakonos* was also held by Paul, Apollos, Epaphras and others. According to its use in some of Paul's other writings and in extra-biblical sources, the term alludes to a missionary dedicated to preaching and teaching.[4] Besides, according to the customs of that time, it was understood that the messenger who carried a letter was well aware of its content and could explain it if necessary. Paul recommends Phoebe in Rom 16: 1-2, while mentioning her titles. She is referred to also as a "protector," "patron" (*prostatis*), a legal term given to those who defended foreigners who have been deprived of their rights. It was a title of honor and authority in ancient times and refers to people to whom others are subordinate. Paul recognized himself to be of lesser status than she. The fact that *diakonos* has been translated as "server" and *prostatis* as "helper" reflects nothing more than the sexist bias of the translators. Being called "sister" denotes, as does "brother," a belonging to a group of missionary coworkers.

Thus Paul entrusts to the hands of Phoebe, a minister of the church in Cenchreae and his coworker and "patron," the letter that would be read out loud to the Christian communities of Rome. Phoebe would then be present to clarify any doubts or questions about its content.

In this same chapter 16 we find in the list of greetings a surprising number of women's names. Of a total of 25 names, 8 belong to women, which, for a document written in androcentric* language, is quite a few. Mentioned next to each name is the work that she has carried out. Unfortunately the active participation of women was gradually eliminated from recorded accounts, as we have noted. Biblical and extra-biblical documents from the end of the first century, and more strongly evident later on, show how women were gradually silenced. The process of exclusion also included the loss of an understanding of the church as a community of equals in every aspect: economically, culturally, ethnically, and by gender. A process of conforming to the structures of Roman imperial society began to take place and corresponding hierarchies appear. The prophetic, radical critique voiced by Jesus and Paul in the face of any kind of oppression begins to be less apparent.[5]

The incorporation of Roman patriarchal social values can be observed in the later biblical texts themselves.[6] One very clear example, cited by Irene Foulkes, is part of the discourse of Titus Livius (first century C.E.). He criticizes the women who had presented themselves in the Roman Forum saying, "What kind of conduct is this?...to speak with the husbands of other wives!..Couldn't you ask your husbands the same questions at home?"[7]

In the New Testament we observe the incorporation of patriarchal ideology in the so-called domestic codes[8] (Col. 3: 18-19; Eph. 5: 21f; 1 Peter 2: 13). These texts and parts of the pastoral letters (1 Tim. 2: 9-15) attempt to regulate women's behavior. We can add to all of this the interpolation* that appears in 1 Cor. 14: 34-35. Here women are commanded to be silent and their exercise of the gift of prophecy is limited.[9] Prohibitions against women's participation in teaching, baptizing, and administering the Lord's Supper continued in later documents. By the end of the post-apostolic period, women were permitted only secondary official functions.[10] The authority of the prophet, whose abilities were understood to be a gift of the Spirit, was eliminated and replaced by that of a bishop. Institutionalization of faith takes place.

It has been said that the negative attitude toward women resulted from the strong external pressure of Greco-Roman society that considered the house-church to be a subversive cell. Therefore if house-churches continued to defy the patriarchal order and values of Roman society, they ran the risk of disappearing completely. This reality, however, doesn't justify the oppression or marginalization of any member of the Christian community. Neither, as Luise Schottroff states, can we legitimize a "patriarchalism of love" because it is still patriarchalism.[11]

Fortunately, the resistance of women continued. The constant repetition of the prohibitions against their participation indicates that women resisted admonitions to be silent in the congregation and to restrictions that eliminated them from leadership roles. They continued to act according to their perception of the Gospel. Like the women of the movement of Jesus in Palestine, they fought for the rights achieved through the new order in Christ. Apocryphal* writings (second century C.E.)[12] show prominent leadership among women. In the third century C.E., Firmilianus, Bishop of Caesarea, mentions a woman from Cappadocia who officiates at the Lord's Supper. In those times of persecution, she courageously gathers the Christian community and includes the Eucharist in their celebration. The astonished bishop says she did it excellently.[13] In the fifth century a bishop is condemned for ordaining women as priests. It seems that the ordination of women had been a generalized phenomenon.[14]

This resistance of women to keeping silent has not stopped right up to today. As Christian women we feel that the Spirit of Jesus and his movement continues to motivate his followers, both women and men, giving them strength and wisdom. Thus the community of equals may carry forward the message of the Kingdom of God and at the same time denounce all that which oppresses and excludes women and any member of the communities.

Notes

1. Paul is not as misogynist as some think. He demonstrated great openness toward women, something we can observe in the closing of his letter to the Romans (chapter 16: 1-16).

2. *Hechos*, p. 273.

3. This section about Phoebe appears in Elsa Tamez, "Der Brief an die Gemeinde in Rom. Eine Feministische Lektüre" in *Kompendium Feministische Bibelauslegung*, Luise Schottroff and Marie-Theresa Wacker, eds. (Güthersloh: Christian Kaiser, 1998), pp. 557-573.

4. Schüssler Fiorenza, *In Memory of Her*, p. 170.

5. See Esperanza Bautista, *La mujer en la iglesia primitiva* (Estella: Verbo Divino, 1993), p. 168.

6. Luise Schottroff's analysis of 1 Tim. 9-15 makes clear that what is happening in Roman society at that time is being duplicated in the early church. Roman society wants to exclude and silence women and the male leaders of the communities behave in the same way. *Lydia's Impatient Sisters*, pp. 70-73.

7. Irene Foulkes, "Conflictos en Corinto. Las mujeres en la iglesia primitiva," in *Revista de Interpretación Bíblica Latinoamericana* (RIBLA), no.15 (1993), p. 107.

8. Most scholars agree that these codes are not from Paul, but were written later, possibly by a disciple of Paul's who used Paul's name in order to give authority to his own writings.

9. No one today doubts that this is an interpolation.* Paul himself is in agreement with women being leaders in the church; to pray and prophesy are signs of leadership. In 1 Cor. 11: 5, he recommends that women pray and prophesy with their heads covered as a sign of decency according to their cultural practice.

10. Suzanne Tunc describes the process of elimination of women's authority in *También las mujeres seguían a Jesús* (Santander: Sal Terrae, 1999), pp. 109-127.

11. Luise Schottroff, *Lydia's Impatient Sisters*, p. 76.

12. The apocryphal book *The Acts of Paul and Thecla*, for example.

13. Suzanne Tunc, *También las mujeres seguían a Jesús*, p. 125.

14. Ibid.

Study Guide

by

Sallie M. Cuffee

Introduction

The introduction to *Jesus and Courageous Women* acquaints us with the fact that far too many women's identities have been all but forgotten and their contribution to salvation history lost. One way women's lives were muted into silence is when special deference to their uniqueness got lost in group identity. In the mind of Luke, for instance, that writer of the third Gospel heralded as sympathetic to women's causes, the women in the Movement did not warrant individual attention but acquired recognition as "certain women" (Luke 8:1-3). To be fair to Luke, he does remember a few of them by name: Mary called Magdalene, Joanna the wife of Chuza, and Susanna. But what of the great many whose names slipped through the cracks of history, forever lost, known only in retrospect by their kind service to Jesus? Yet Luke's inclusion of them acknowledges that they were there. Clearly his diplomatic concession to female presence invites those early women into the public eye of history. Acknowledged by author Elsa Tamez, "Generally, when women are included in history, the fact that they are mentioned at all is more significant than it would first appear."

By and large the names and stories of women's lives suffer the burden of history's amnesia. For any quick survey of biblical history will reveal that few of those first-century female disciples enjoyed the prominence accorded their male colleagues. Ask anyone to name the disciples of Jesus and one is apt to hear immediately Peter, James, John, Andrew and the other eight male disciples. To my mind, the absence of women in that roster is painfully glaring. Indeed, from my perspective women in the Movement of Jesus gain entry into public consciousness more from the suspicion surrounding their invisibility in Scripture than because of their actual presence in recorded biblical accounts.

The visible presence of women at the cross, however, gives significant witness. During that ordeal, the women in the life of

Jesus were there—bewildered, yes; suffering the despair of loss in the moment, of course; but daring in their caring and loving at the same time. To simply be there amid obviously hostile conditions, they risked the threat of bodily harm from Roman soldiers as they mourned the loss of a beloved teacher, friend, and leader in a mutual seeking of spiritual truth and in the struggle for just relations (see Matthew 27: 55-56; Mark 15: 40-41; Luke 23: 27; John 19: 25).

At the crucifixion and the resurrection, women emerge as the true disciples. They remain steadfastly with Jesus. They are the ones commissioned as the authentic bearers of a new vision of community, a community irrevocably in conflict with the oppressive values of a pre-Easter Sunday world. Their legacy lives on. Down through the centuries, women have been beneficiaries of the efforts of those early women who followed Jesus to preach and act on a life-altering message that promised spiritual empowerment and social transformation. That same message holds inspiration for women and men today. This study offers yet another witness to and opportunity to learn from the moral courage of those women who were important participants in biblical history.

PREPARING TO BE A STUDY LEADER

An effective study leader creates an environment where participants contribute to each session, so that everyone is both a learner and a leader. As leader in this study, you will guide others in looking at the lives of women in the Movement of Jesus, the Christ. No doubt, some will have more experience and knowledge than you do. But, as leader, your best strategy is to spend as much time as you can on preparation. Your responsibility is to guide the class, not to establish yourself as the authority over either the class or the subject matter. If you see yourself as a well-prepared facilitator rather than an expert, each participant in your class will be empowered to learn. The leader also sets the tone for group participation, encouraging group members to take an active part in group discussion and activity to their own level of comfort.

Steps for Study Leaders

1. Ask God's assistance in prayer.
2. Create an affirming atmosphere. Remember to love your class members, pray for them, and affirm each person and each contribution a class member makes. Use words like "Yes!" "That's good," "Say more," "That's helpful," and, of course, "Thank you."
3. Consider introducing sessions with important points from your own reading and experience, while offering time for participants to share their thoughts.
4. Read as many of the books listed in the Selected Bibliography on page 173 as possible. Check with your local church pastor or local public library for some of these excellent resources. *The New Interpreter's Bible* (Leander Keck, ed. Nashville: Abingdon Press, 1994; 12 vols.) and *The Women's Bible Commentary* (C. Newsom and S. Ringe [Louisville: Westminster John Knox Press, 1992]) give excellent biblical background and interpretation.
5. Read the basic text and the Study Guide closely. Be sure to make notes as you read of important points or issues to cover, and include examples from your own experience to add to the class discussion.
6. Create an outline for each session. It may be helpful to assign a time frame for each part of the session (10 minutes, 30 minutes, etc.). As your study progresses, you may alter your session plans to accommodate the interests and needs of the group. It is always helpful to work through each session, including amounts of time for each segment so you know approximately the flow of the session. Be detailed and flexible. If the class "comes together" as a group, there will be suggestions from individuals and the group as a whole as to specific direction for the later sessions. Create a simplified outline for class participants. Hand out copies or write it on newsprint or on overhead transparencies. In this way, the class understands where all of you are headed.
7. Learning activities are created for any number of audiences that may be using this material. Our purpose is to consider the needs of the local unit as well as those preparing to participate in Schools of Christian Mission. So you may not cover

every activity. Choose the ones that best fulfill the goals. As study leader, you may select activities appropriate to your context.

8. Arrange for any special supplies, sources materials or equipment needed for each session well before your group gathers. Arrange the room setting appropriately for each session.

9. Make use of the computer's Internet. If you do not have Internet access at home, call your library, church, college or computer friend. They will be happy to help you. If you are not familiar with computers, arrange for someone to be a mentor for the class. If there is a computer lab accessible to your class, or a library with ample computer access nearby, you may want to arrange to use these facilities. Or if you are on a weekly schedule for this study, plan a field trip to your library or computer lab. If you are presenting this study in a college setting, students are usually on duty to supervise the computer lab and can provide excellent assistance.

10. Look ahead to decide which Web site materials you will want to use. Check the Selected Bibliography on page 173 for Web site listings. **Important: Please observe all copyright restrictions on the Web sites and follow requirements there for reproducing materials.** You could access all of the Web sites during one sitting, then print out hard copies of the material you will be using. Then put together a booklet of these excerpts that can be placed on a resource table or copied for each participant at your local photocopying shop. Some particularly useful sites:

For the Women's Division Web site for this study, see:
http://gbgm-umc.org/umw/jesusandwomen/

For the Women's Division Web site on the spiritual growth study on Corinthians, see:
http://gbgm-umc.org/umw/corinthians
You can also click on several useful maps here.

For the General Commission on the Status and Role of Women (COSROW) Web site:
http://www.umc.org/gcsrw

(Also check the lists of Online Resources in the 2001 study book *Conflict and Community in the Corinthian Church* for more sites on church communities in the New Testament period; see pages 71 and 120.)

11. Give regular assignments. After each session, assignments are noted for the next class. Go over the assignments before the closing worship each day. If at all possible, assign chapter one in the study text before the first session. If this is not possible, add chapter one to the assignment for Session II.

PREPARATION FOR ALL SESSIONS

1. Be sure enough United Methodist hymnals or other songbooks are available for participants. Or, for large group use, request permission from the copyright holders to copy hymns for worship during all sessions.
2. This study book *Jesus and Courageous Women* by Elsa Tamez with Study Guide by Sallie M. Cuffee is the basic text. Encourage each class member to purchase a copy, or provide copies at the first session. Announce that specific reading assignments will be made for each session. (See page 182 for ordering information.)
3. Ask group participants to bring their Bibles to each class session. Encourage the use of various translations (King James, New Revised Standard, New International Version, etc.) to compare and contrast wording for each passage used. Also, provide several Bibles in different translations. Be creative! Ask several members to present a dramatic reading of Scripture, or read the verses antiphonally, dividing the group into sections. Or try a simple liturgical dance or roleplay.
4. Sessions one through five are planned for a two-hour schedule. Each session is put in a context of worship and study. Please begin and end each session with a prayer and Scripture reading even if no other worship form is used. Ahead of time, assign readers for Scripture and other leader roles during worship.

5. Encourage participants to keep a journal throughout this study. Journaling may include responses to the Scripture references in each chapter of the study book or questions or activities in the Study Guide. Participants may also want to record their thoughts, feelings, simple drawings or symbols, and insights about the stories of Jesus and the women. Encourage participants with questions such as: "In what ways do you identify with or find inspiration from a particular woman's story?" "What insights have you gained about Jesus or a particular woman disciple?" "What feelings do you experience in response to a courageous woman's life situation?"

6. Provide a suggestion box or notebook for participants to use daily. Time probably will not allow for all to speak or to make their suggestions known, and this box or book is a way each individual can contribute. It also affords the opportunity to speak up anonymously if desired. This also encourages ownership of the group process by everyone.

7. Purchase a copy of the *Youth Study–Jesus and Courageous Women* (#2967, $4.75). Illustrations appear in it for many of the stories about Jesus and women. See page 182 for complete ordering information.

Classroom Setting: Be sure the room size allows for the comfortable participation of your group.

1. *Arrangement of the Meeting Room:* Try to meet in a room that allows an informal setting. Placing chairs in a circle, a semicircle or concentric circle encourages participation. Make sure that people with mobility impairments, reduced sight and hearing find the best places for their participation. Make sure the room is large enough for the number of people anticipated, with space to move chairs around in different configurations. Check that the room temperature is comfortable and that you know how to adjust it. Know the location of the nearest rest rooms and build comfort breaks into your teaching plans. The space should also allow for gathering in smaller activity centers and discussion groups.

2. *Resources:* Provide a resource table that contains as many of the suggested books and materials as possible, as well as others you have found. If you have access to the Internet, download materials from the appropriate Web sites. Compile these pages into a booklet which will be available for special assignments or additional reading.

3. *Supplies:* Arrange for a chalkboard and chalk, or an easel with newsprint pad and lots of markers for large and small group use and visibility. Plan ahead to make sufficient supplies available for each session and keep them in one place. Arrange for a monitor and VCR if you plan to use videos. Be sure the room can be darkened and locate outlets. Bring an extension cord for all electrical equipment. You will need several large sheets of brown packing paper or shelf paper and wall space for the "Courageous Women Quilt" and the "Open Community Wall" described in Sessions II and III.

4. *The Setting:* Create an attractive and welcoming room by decorating the space according to your taste; use maps, illustrations, and photos that help participants grasp women in the Movement of Jesus, the Christ, and generally in church and society within the context of the study. Using material from Web sites will be helpful. Members of the group might be asked to bring symbols of their faith to be left in the room. Set aside a table or a portion of the meeting space to serve as "sacred space" or "holy of holies." The focus of this space can change for each session, perhaps to reflect the particular courageous women who will be the focus of the session, or as the group desires. A piano or keyboard would be useful for the worship times.

Some ideas to consider:
- Gather dry grass, small bare branches, and leaves, a flower or little stones—to symbolize God's creation. Such symbols keep before us those who are left silent and voiceless in our community. As we lift them up and give them a place of honor when we gather, we affirm God's love for each of us and that

God's creation is intricately interwoven with the natural world and all humanity as family.

- Collect grains from which bread is made. Different grains are used in different cultures or different parts of the world. Rice, corn meal, wheat, barley, and rye are some. These grains represent a major responsibility of women around the world–food cultivation and preparation. The key feeding and nurturing responsibilities of women also include the major part women play in sowing and cultivating seeds of faith in their communities. Their presence symbolizes the invitation to all the world to come to God's table without exception or human preference.
- Bring candles, water, incense, containers—symbolizing God's Spirit among us. Set these items among the others to represent God's empowering presence.
- Include photos, pictures, and sketches of women important to us or significant in biblical or church history. This portrayal of women makes them visible and brings their stories alive for the nurturing of the community.
- Encourage the group to be creative. For each session, ask for suggestions of symbols that tie in with the texts or themes, or examples from their life experiences that are relevant to the group's study at that time. This will help build ownership of the learning process.

Announcements and Assignments:
Begin each session with a time for announcements that might include ideas, insights, and suggestions from group members about the study, upcoming church and community events, and mission projects in which the group might participate. Before the closing worship, review the assignments for the next session that would include: the text and Scripture readings; additional materials to be read, special reports or presentations, newspaper articles to collect, movies or TV shows to view, special music or worship elements, volunteer worship leaders, etc.

Women and the Movement of Jesus, the Christ

Purpose: To set the framework and context of the study

Objectives for This Session
- To restore the visible presence of women to the public ministry of Jesus and to the Christian Church
- To introduce the social and political context of the Movement of Jesus
- To bring into contemporary discussion the relevance of the Movement of Jesus
- To engage participants in the process of interpretation called Midrash*

Preparing for the Session
1. Encourage participants to read the Introduction in the text before the first session.
2. Provide materials for the Community-Building activities: name-tags (or colored paper and markers and pins for making them); pens and paper for letter-writing.
3. Display maps for the review of biblical geography and the historic sites presented in the session; or enlarge the maps on the Women's Division Web site or its links.
4. Select specific resources—art, posters, photos, artifacts, or

anecdotal details—to bring biblical geography alive.
5. Provide *The United Methodist Hymnal.*
6. Duplicate "A Biblical Inventory" for each participant.

A Biblical Inventory

1. Who is the first prophet mentioned in the New Testament? (Luke 2: 36-38) *Anna*
2. Who are some of Jesus' disciples (not the 12!) who gave their own money to help support Jesus' ministry? (Luke 8: 1-3)
3. Who were the first people to see Jesus alive after the Resurrection? (Matt. 28: 1-10) *Mary Magdalene, Mary - Mother*
4. Who were some of the other disciples of Jesus besides the 12? (Mark 15: 40-41)
5. Who was the first non-Jew to tell others about Jesus? (John 4: 27-30, 39) *Woman from Samaria*
6. Who was a teacher and leader in the early Christian church who probably wrote the Letter to the Hebrews (it wasn't Paul!)? (Acts 18: 2-26; Rom. 16: 3)

—Adapted from Alyson Huntly, "The Impossibly Difficult Bible Quiz," *Worldview* 10, no.1 (1991): 12. From Worldview 1992. The United Church of Canada. Reprinted with permission.

Gathering Time

1. Invite participants to make a name-tag as they arrive.
2. Hand out "A Biblical Inventory." Ask participants to answer the questions individually or in pairs. Encourage them to answer as many as they can and to skip the questions they cannot answer. Hold on to the handout for discussion later in the session.
3. Ask participants to prepare to share background information about themselves, their interests, their spiritual journeys, and the relationship each has within The United Methodist Church or another church community.

Announcements

Opening Worship

Hymn: #277, "Tell Me the Stories of Jesus," *The United Methodist Hymnal*, verse 1

Scripture: Mark 3: 31-35; Matthew 12: 46-50; Luke 8: 19-21

Prayer
You call us into discipleship,
O One Who Bears All Burdens,
making a way through the wilderness,
hovering near in pillar and cloud,
revealing bits of Your glory
when all seems hopeless
and courage fails.
Carry us on the wingtips of Your
never-failing promise,
through moments of discouragement
as we push against the tide.
You are my friends,
You told us all,
my friends and my disciples.
Be with us always,
be with us now
as we seek Your way.
Amen.

—Miriam Therese Winter in *WomanWord: A Feminist Lectionary and Psalter, Women of the New Testament*, p. 153. Copyright © 1991. All rights reserved. Used with permission of The Crossroad Publishing Company, New York.

Hymn: #277, "Tell Me the Stories of Jesus," *The United Methodist Hymnal*, verses 2 and 3

Activity:
Sharing About Yourself
Invite participants to gather in pairs to become familiar with each other's names. As individuals feel comfortable, ask them to share with each other about their own local "context," including bits of background information about their locale, social status, profession, family, spiritual journey, and what role they play in their local church, and perhaps in their community. (This process will provide an opportunity for participants to reflect later on aspects of their own social status and context in relation to women in Jesus' day.) Ask the pairs to introduce each other to the rest of the group by sharing information with respect for the comfort level of the other.

Introducing the Study

Women refuse to relegate the Jesus story to a story only about men. It's also a story about women, although different traditions and some biblical writers appear devoted to minimizing this point or arguing it otherwise. Sometimes the stories handed down did not include women and children at all. Generally when women are mentioned in association with Jesus, it is because biblical writers were explicitly obliged to acknowledge feminine presence. In stories that detail the death, burial and resurrection of Jesus, for example, women are accorded special consideration because of their demonstrated strong, visible presence. And yet, how do we explain that the names of the same women keep cropping up throughout readings of the Movement of Jesus? Are they simply token references? Or is this really indicative of the limited involvement of women rather than of any obvious bias on the part of the male authors? I think not. In many instances, it emphasizes the significance of their position and commitment to Jesus' nascent movement. But, in a real sense, they are also those who narrowly escaped the amnesia of a male reading of biblical history. That explains why the subject of the study book by Elsa Tamez, *Jesus and Courageous Women*, requires readers to probe beneath the surface of anonymity and discover the unique, significant contribution that individual women brought to the Movement of Jesus.

General Outline for the Study

Present and discuss the general outline of the study. Ask what participants hope to learn. Introduce the basic resources, emphasizing that each member needs a study book and a Bible. Introduce additional materials that are placed on the resource table. Invite class members to add materials to that table. Point out the suggestion box or notebook and how participants are to use it. Also encourage journaling throughout the study to help participants connect the women's stories to their own spiritual journey and personal context. Allow time for general questions and comments.

Learning Activities

1. **Women and the Movement of Jesus: A Biblical Inventory.** The biblical inventory on page 114 begins our study into the lives of the women involved in the Movement of Jesus, the Christ. The inventory gives us some insight about our biblical knowledge about women who accompanied Jesus and 12 male disciples. Who comes to mind when you think about disciples, teachers, apostles, and prophets in the Bible? Men or women? Refer to the inventory. Review each question and the group's responses. Ask for volunteers to read aloud to the group the Scripture references with each question. Inquire as to why we do not know many facts about these New Testament biblical women. Explore ways to restore within local churches the visible presence of women in biblical and church history.

2. **Setting the Context that Gave Birth to the Jesus Movement.** Give a description of the social and political conditions of the birthplace of the movement in Galilee. Name the prominent cities and the significance "Lydia," the narrator, attaches to them. Ask participants if any have traveled in the Middle East and to the specific places in the Introduction. If so, what was their experience? What geographical sites and features held their attention and why? Then move to how Jesus felt about cities. Was he more comfortable in rural, agricultural centers? Why? How does Jesus' geographical and

social location affect, frame, and influence his ministry? (Use the map on the Women's Division Web site to point out the geographical region and key cities that defined Jesus' travels.)

3. **The Narrative Technique.** Note that author Elsa Tamez uses the biblical woman "Lydia" to introduce and narrate the facts and stories of the early Movement of Jesus, the Christ. Conduct an interview in the first person of "I, Lydia." Stage it as though this interview is being broadcast live directly from Philippi by using the pages of the Introduction in the text. Begin with who she is and her interest in telling the story of the Movement of Jesus, the Christ. Include the facts in Acts 16: 11-15, 40. Use these questions to guide the content of the interview:
   • What is the significance of you as a woman telling this history?
   • What was it about the Movement of Jesus that gives you the authority to speak?
   • Why are you concerned about men only writing the history of the Movement of Jesus?
   • What did you learn about Jesus?

4. **Women Creating Their Own "Midrash."** Note to the class that "I, Lydia," is writing her own Midrash. The term "midrash" is defined as an imagined or projected story based on biblical events that might have happened on a particular occasion. The point of midrash is to enhance or clarify the underlying meaning of a Bible story or text. "Lydia" is telling the story of the Movement of Jesus, the Christ through her eyes. Because women receive the Gospel knowledge of women through male writers, here is an opportunity for participants to express their own Gospel understanding. As individuals or in groups of two's, express in writing, image, or role play a "midrash" of a female encounter with the Movement of Jesus, as told in her voice. For this activity, Lydia can be selected as one model. Based upon the information provided in the Introduction, her thoughts and feelings could be further developed. Also, consider other female personalities included in the Introduction or imagine one.

Include the emotional dimension to your storytelling. In other words, how did it feel being there? What did you discover about yourself? About the Movement? About Jesus? Is Jesus chastised or praised for his involvement with women? Why or why not? Be creative. Encourage use of visual art, poetry, song, a litany or letter format.

5. **A Group Sharing of "Midrashim."** Bring the entire class together to share the individual or group presentations. Post around the room any visual art, poems, litanies, songs, or letters to keep women's experience before everyone.

6. **Exploring Terms.** Explore with class members the term "the Movement of Jesus, the Christ." How does Lydia define it? What distinguishes it from the term "Christianity"? Make two columns on newsprint. Label one: "the Movement of Jesus" and the other "Christianity." Note responses. Perhaps expand the discussion: are there contemporary examples that come to mind of a "Movement of Jesus, the Christ" in our nation, within our churches and/or faith-based communities? Discuss their special characteristics. Who are among the members and why?

Assignments for Session II

1. Assign the reading of Part I, "Women Who Love and Dare," chapters 1-3 in the text for the next session.

2. Ask the group to come prepared to write, paint, and or draw the name(s) of biblical, historical, and contemporary courageous women whom they believe acted to challenge patriarchal power. If they have pictures and/or photos, that would be an appropriate addition. Explain that the individual squares will be arranged on a paper or cloth surface in a quilt design with the idea of "stitching" together women's lives under the theme "Courageous Women."

3. Ask for a volunteer to explore aspects of the role of women in Jewish and Roman patriarchal societies. Check the Web sites

on pages 177-79, especially Diotima,
http://www.stoa.org/diotima

The First Christians: Roles for Women:
http://www.pbs.org/wgbh/pages/frontline/shows/
   religion/first/roles.html

Palestine in the Time of Jesus: Social Structures and Social
Conflicts:
http://www.stolaf.edu/people/kchanson/ptj.html

4. Ask three class participants to volunteer to do close back-
    ground reading on Mary, the Mother of Jesus; Mary and
    Martha; and the Woman Almost Stoned. Use the Selected
    Bibliography on page 173 for additional source material.
    What interpretation(s) of these women's lives do they discov-
    er? They will each resource one of the three small groups
    assigned to reread the specific biblical presentations of these
    women's stories.

Closing Worship

Hymn: #143, "On Eagle's Wings," *The United Methodist Hymnal*

Divide the group to read alternately the following:

Responsive Reading or Litany: "A Psalm of Spirit"

> **Choir 1:** Come, Holy Spirit,
> rattle the rooms in which we are hiding,
> shake the tired foundations
> until the institution crumbles,
> break the rules
> that keep You out of all our
> sacred spaces,
> then lift from the dust and rubble
> a completely new creation.

Choir 2: Come, Holy Spirit,
enter our lives,
whisper our names
and scatter Your gifts of grace
with wild abandon,
give Your silent strength to all imprisoned
by the structures,
and let Your raging fire be our song
of liberty.

All: Come, Holy Spirit,
help us find ourselves
in vital places,
bringing Your word of freedom
to the poor and the oppressed.
We will remember
women were there
when You burst upon a waiting world
creating and recreating
opportunities
for everyone
to feel and fear
Your face.

—Miriam Therese Winter in *WomanWord: A Feminist Lectionary and Psalter, Women of the New Testament,* p. 38. Copyright © 1991. All rights reserved. Used with permission of The Crossroad Publishing Company, New York.

Hymn: #143, "On Eagle's Wings," *The United Methodist Hymnal*

Women Who Love
and Dare

Purpose: To bring into historical focus the names and identities of women around Jesus

Objectives for This Session:
- To discover the identity of four particular women who were part of the Movement of Jesus
- To introduce the term "patriarchy" and its relationship to power in the context of women's lives
- To examine women's roles in the Movement of Jesus and women's roles in local churches and communities

Preparing for the Session
1. Provide small squares (about 5" x 5") cut out of colored construction paper. Have crayons, paints, and markers for decorating "quilting" squares. Bring a long sheet of shelf or brown packing paper and glue for mounting the squares. Locate wall space to hang the "quilt."
2. Write the definition of "patriarchy" found in the Glossary (page 172) on newsprint and post where it is clearly visible.
3. Refer to Elisabeth Schüssler Fiorenza's book *In Memory of Her*, specifically the chapter "The Jesus Movement as Renewal Movement Within Judaism." (See the Selected Bibliography on page 175.)
4. Provide newsprint sheets to use for large group discussion of emerging portraits of women.

5. Provide *The United Methodist Hymnal* and extra Bibles for class use.

Announcements

Opening Worship

Hymn: #198, "My Soul Gives Glory to My God," *The United Methodist Hymnal*, verses 1 and 2

Scripture: Luke 10: 38-42; John 11: 1-15, 12: 1-8

Prayer: #489, "For God's Gifts," *The United Methodist Hymnal*

Hymn: #198, "My Soul Gives Glory to My God," *The United Methodist Hymnal*, verses 3 and 4

Introduction to the Session

In this session, our task requires no less than reconstructing the silent lives of women who were members of the Movement of Jesus, the Christ. Given the cultural limitations faced by the women, the task of reconstructing their lives cannot be accomplished within the scope of this study. There are three female personalities who assume classic import: Mary, the Mother of Jesus and Martha and Mary, intimate friends of Jesus. While their names feel so familiar and their stories well-known from Sunday school retelling, they are probably better known from what we imagine about them than from what biblical narrative actually reports about their lives.

"Lydia" assists us ably with our present task. Through her eyes, women's identities and their important contribution are partially restored to salvation history. We regain an enormous sense of women's risk-taking activities to ensure their inclusion. Salvation history reveals women were instrumental, if not critical, to the success of the Movement of Jesus. Beyond fund-raising to ensure the financial security of the Movement, women were the last standing with Jesus at his death and the first to visit his tomb. Women proved able eyewitnesses to the resurrection and confident evangelists of the commission: "Go, tell his disciples" (Mark 16: 7). The first chapters of our study indicate unequivocally that the Movement of Jesus inspired the participation of courageous women and men.

Learning Activities

1. Power Study: Patriarchy. A. Ask for definitions, characteristics, and attitudes from the class. Write some on the newsprint. Post the definition from the Glossary. Explain patriarchy so that it gets at issues of male power over women. Then define sexism; a general definition would be discrimination against women based on gender. Link it to the violent manifestations of that power that range from women's loss of control of their bodies and their identity to naming themselves. Extend the discussion to the overt violence of rape, domestic violence, and the many expressions of institutional oppression of women. In this power analysis, the participants should consider:
- language that is exclusive and male-identified, such as in liturgies, sermons, and the generic use of "man" to refer to humanity;
- how women and men are stereotyped by adjectives and pronouns that carry value judgments;
- the low self-esteem and diminished self-value that women feel which encourages personal and institutional violence;
- how concepts of "power over" rather than "power with" emerge and dominate behaviors;
- how women respond to and create survival strategies in a patriarchal and hierarchical world.

B. For healing. Use this exercise to lead to the healing of women and men. The healing ritual builds upon the assumption that patriarchy has fundamentally been a form of domination and violence against women. The class can produce its own litany of freedom or use the one prepared below. Begin by reciting Psalm 22: A Prayer of Lamentation. Then decide how best to recite the litany below as a group.

Group Litany

We are here to end patriarchal violence. Yes, we will!

We are here to break the terror. Yes, we will!
We are here to heal the wounded. Yes, we will!
We are here to help each other. Yes, we will!
We are here to make a new beginning. Yes, we will!
We are here to change the system. Yes, we will!
We are moving out together. Yes, we are!
We are creating a new world that is safe and happy. Yes, we are!
Where women, men and children can live together without fear.
    Yes, we will!
The end of the old, the beginning of the new. This is the time!
The end of terror, the beginning of safety. This is the place!
The end of silence. The beginning of protest and change.
We are the ones, and we will do it. Yes, we will!

—from *Ecumenical Decade, 1988-1998, Churches in Solidarity with Women: Prayers and poems, songs, and stories*, WCC Publications, Geneva, 150 route de Ferney, 1211 Geneva 20, Switzerland

2. Women Around Jesus. The women listed below are identified according to how the Gospel portrays them. Some of them are mentioned only according to a traditional relationship they share with a male partner or relative. For others, the Gospel writers appear more interested in highlighting their female condition or the sensual nature of their state that provoked their encounter with Jesus. Few receive recognition for their own identity and in their own right. In spite of that cultural baggage, how did the actions of these women challenge cultural patterns that pre-scribed female subordination? Ask the volunteer who did reading on women's role in a Jewish and Roman world to make a brief (5-10 minute) report or share comments.

A listing of "Certain Women" Around Jesus:
Mary Magdalene (John 20:1-18)
Sisters of Jesus (Matthew 13: 54-58)
Joanna, the wife of Chuza (Luke 24: 1-25)
Susanna (Luke 8: 1-3)
Mary, the mother of Jesus (Luke 1: 26-56; 2: 1-52)
Mary, the wife of Clopas (John 19: 25-27)
Mary and Martha (John 12:1-8; Luke 10:38-42)

Some of the unnamed women:

The woman with an issue of blood (Mark 5: 25-34; Luke 8: 43-48; Matthew 9: 20-22)

The woman with five husbands (John 4: 1-42)

The woman who anointed Jesus' feet (Mark 14: 3-9; Matthew 26: 6-13)

The woman accused of adultery (John 8: 2-11)

A daughter of a Canaanite woman possessed by an evil spirit (Mark 7: 24-30; Matthew 15: 21-28)

Divide the class into four or five small groups, based on the size of the class. Assign each group task A or B below. Encourage them to use the material in the Introduction and chapter 1 in the text. Ask each group to present its topic to the rest of the class in a creative format, such as roleplay, a skit or a dramatic monologue created by each group.

A. Select a specific woman from either list and present a description of her from the viewpoint of the culture of that time. Include the woman's social status and/or profession, if known. Refer to quotes from the Scripture passages cited as necessary. Consider the woman from the perspective of a male disciple, a Jewish critic, a Roman authority, or a male family member. Attempt to get at some of the issues of power and control that defined female and male relationships.

B. Choose a specific woman from the list and present a description of her from the viewpoint of a woman who made the choice to be in ministry to Jesus or who was ministered to by Jesus. Include the woman's status and/or profession, if known. Lift up likely obstacles and barriers that she may have encountered when she moved beyond the boundaries of the traditional social sphere prescribed for women. Ask: were any of these women mothers? What does it mean to be an itinerant and a mother? What did the women sacrifice in terms of family, friends, and community? How would society judge her? Relate that to today's female itinerant ministers or pastors, who are also mothers and members of families and communities today. Mary is the dominant image of mother emphasized in the Gospels. How are the issues and concerns Mary faced similar to or different from other mothers of her time? Of today?

3. A Reflection/Journaling Exercise. The focus shifts here to looking at women's relationships: how has patriarchal society constructed female relationships toward one another? In addition to external factors as a source of female oppression, women must also evaluate how we undermine one another in a hierarchically organized world where women are subordinate to men. How does the mother image, so warmly and compassionately made synonymous with Mary, the mother of Jesus, serve as a two-edged sword? Can it not be used to empower or disempower women, especially when she is young, single, pregnant, and unemployed? What are the choices? What factors are at play in using the mother image? The many faces of Mary are rarely explored or exposed.

How do women overcome the social competitiveness encouraged among us? For example, how can Mary and Martha represent models of women who have different gifts to offer to the church community without their being in competition with each other? Do we welcome the offering of different gifts and create opportunities for their expression and integration into the life of the church? Refer to Romans 12: 5-8. Think of yourself and your gifts. Then think of gifts not included in the listing.

Or, consider the woman without a female companion to stand in solidarity with her. She stands alone, accused of adultery before her male accusers. Does, or should, any woman ever have to stand alone against the onslaught of patriarchal domination? Her fight should be the fight of all women. And it is! Every woman should have at least one "sister" to depend upon. Think of situations where women feel alone and alienated, e.g., divorce, single-parenting, domestic abuse, rape, molestation, sexual harassment, etc. How does your local unit respond to women in these situations? How could a local unit respond to reach out in an education and consciousness-raising campaign?

4. Four Female Personalities in the Movement.
A. Mary, Mother of Jesus, Leader of the Movement (Luke 1: 26-56)
B. Martha and Mary, Friends of Jesus (Luke 10: 38-42;
    John 11: 1-15; 12: 1-8)
C. The Woman Who Was Not Stoned According to the Law
    (John 8: 3-11)
Divide into three groups. Assign to each group one of the person-

alities listed above. Ask each group to read those selected portions of Scripture. Consider these questions: What is the good news in this passage? The bad news? What new insight or understanding emerges? How do you relate this passage to your own life? Then, ask each group to reinterpret its Scripture passages. Imagine being another woman character in the story. How would you react to what was happening? Center on "sister-strength," which means nothing less than "being present" with one another. Decide how best to express the interpretation: through dance, music, movement, art, gestures of solidarity, a letter to the "sister." Encourage each group to integrate its responses with the queries raised in the Reflection/Journaling activity. Bring the entire class together to share group presentations. List insights and surprises.

5. Women's Roles Today. As a total group, ask for impressions that underscore differences and similarities among women's roles in contemporary church and society and the biblical context. Also give attention to actions women have taken to overcome obstacles and hardships in these biblical stories and today in the church. Write on newsprint the participants' responses and post around the room. What portraits emerge of women? What are their strengths? How have faith and courage been demonstrated? How have new images of women contributed to the ordination and appointment of female pastors, and the election and designation of bishops, and lay leaders in the church? What leadership roles do women hold in your local church? In your annual conference? See the Selected Bibliography on page 173 for helpful resources.

6. A "Courageous Women Quilt." Toward the end of the session, ask the group to write, paint, or draw the names on a quilting square of a biblical, historical, or contemporary courageous woman who they believe acted to challenge patriarchal power and, in the process, re-empowered women's memory. Make visible their identities. Include names from international leadership, Bible stories, United States history, United Methodist tradition, or one's personal history. Honor these women. Use the names, photos, and pictures of these women to create a "Courageous Women quilt." Make it colorful. The quilt will keep names before the group throughout the course of this study. Individuals may be as creative as possible and add to the quilt throughout the study. See the Selected Bibliography on page 173 for helpful resources.

Assignments for Session III

- Assign Part II, "Women Who Struggle and Resist," chapters 4-6 in the text for the next session.
- Ask group members to bring an item symbolic of the gifts women in the Gospel stories bring to the Jesus community. Or, items that symbolize their own gifts to the "open community" or "church without walls." Ask them to stretch their imagination, so that items from nature will be included. (Note: The Jesus community is an open community, a church without walls.)
- Briefly explain the concept of an "open community" to the class. Then review the questions in Session III in Activity 1. Ask class members to begin to note responses to questions posed in the next session in their journals.
- Ask for volunteers to participate in the opening and closing worship and give them assignments.

Closing Worship

Hymn: #274, "Woman in the Night," *The United Methodist Hymnal*, verses 1 and 2

Stories of Empowerment (Ask for volunteers to share some brief stories of the women who've empowered, inspired, or encouraged them.)

Ritual of Naming (Some may wish to call aloud the names of a woman important to him or her.)

Affirmation of Faith: #886, *The United Methodist Hymnal*

Hymn: #274, "Woman in the Night," *The United Methodist Hymnal*, verses 3 and 4

Women Who Struggle and Resist

Purpose: To introduce women's everyday experience as justice work for achieving moral community

Objectives for This Session
- To use biblical stories of women's everyday lives as a resource for analysis of unjust social structures
- To understand and value open community or the "church without walls" as a Christian ideal
- To look at practices that create and sustain open community
- To encourage solidarity with women's justice activities

Preparing for the Session
1. Tape a few pieces of newsprint together or a large sheet of brown packing paper on a wall. (Be sure the ink from markers will not bleed through onto the surface below!) With a heavy-tip marker, draw oblong blocks representing building blocks. Make the shapes large enough to write words or phrases inside. Provide colored markers or crayons.
2. Set up an easel with newsprint or a chalkboard.
3. Cover a table with a cloth that represents another area of the world or an indigenous people.
4. Place on the table a large pottery jug, pitcher, bowl, or vase; or

prepare a drawing of a large, Middle Eastern water jar such as might have been used by the Samaritan woman at Jacob's Well.

5. Provide *The United Methodist Hymnal* and extra Bibles.

Announcements

Opening Worship

Hymn: #274, "Woman in the Night," *The United Methodist Hymnal*, verses 5 and 6

Scripture: Proverbs 14: 31; Exodus 22: 21-22; Prov. 17: 5; 15: 25; 19: 17; 22: 22-23

Opening Prayer

> God of Hope and Justice, we know you walk beside us.
> We want to act on your behalf, but we are afraid.
> Give us the courage to be agents of change,
> to challenge the status quo,
> to resist injustice and inequality.
> May your liberating love free us
> to find and use our voices.
> You have given us in your grace and mercy
> the tools to rebuild;
> now empower us with the courage to begin.
> In the name of our brother, Jesus, we pray. Amen.

> —Adapted from a prayer by Julie Howard in *We Are the Circle: Celebrating the Feminine in Song and Ritual* (Collegeville, Minn.: The Liturgical Press, 1993), p. 17. Used by permission.

Hymn: #274, "Woman in the Night," *The United Methodist Hymnal*, verses 7 and 8

Introduction to the Session

We focus on the justice-making activities of women. These activities directly relate to the strenuous efforts required to build an "open community," that is, a just community or a "church without walls." Lydia remarks that what she likes about the "movement of Jesus is that there is respect for all persons and, even more, there is special consideration given to the marginalized" (p. 49). Everyone in the "open community" is a person of worth. The Movement of Jesus is our model of an open community. It challenged many patriarchal practices of Greco-Roman culture that had closed its doors to the marginalized, as our own culture does today.

Learning Activities

Activity 1:
The "Open Community"

With the entire group, review pages 43-50 in the text. Using the material there and the summary below, explain the meaning of "open community." Why was it so liberating when practiced by Jesus?

"Open Community" is defined as a community that welcomes all regardless of race, gender, class, ethnicity–or any distinction that could separate people from each other. Within its circle, all people are treated equally as children of God. In the Gospels we learn that Jesus sought out sinners, publicans and tax collectors, slaves, freed slaves, the ill and outcast. He offered acceptance, forgiveness, and community.

1. Ask the group to divide into pairs or small groups and discuss:
- What cultural and social factors in Jesus' time led to the marginalization of the poor, women and children, or the ill ? How were they excluded? Encourage use of the study text and the Scripture stories there.
- Then turn to your local community: Who are the poor and marginalized? What social and cultural conditions encourage oppression and exclusion in the community?
- Next, think about situations when you felt like the outsider,

marginalized or excluded. What was the situation?

- Finally, consider your local church: Is it closed to "outsiders"? Who are they? How does your church exclude people? Have you ever felt marginalized or excluded within your local church? How might these issues be addressed? What changes must occur? What values and practices would your church lift up to work toward the goal of inclusion within and outside its walls? Encourage each pair or group to list brief responses to each question on newsprint.

2. Come together as a total group. Ask each pair or small group to identify for the class those groups or individuals who have been actively or passively excluded from local and church communities. How would they be invited in? What specific steps or concrete action must be taken?

3. Direct attention to the "building blocks" drawn on the newsprint. This represents a symbolic foundation essential to the creation of an open community. Ask the group to call out words or phrases that characterize the Gospel women highlighted in chapters 1-6 in the text. Words might include attributes such as : faith, willingness to risk one's life or reputation; vision; wisdom; seekers of truth; commitment; daring; boldness; challengers of oppressive law and tradition; breaking out of anonymity; strength; trust; discipleship; witness; courage; persistence; humility, etc. Explain that these qualities are essential building blocks for the open community of the Movement of Jesus—the "church without walls," God's just society.

Activity 2:
Women Witness Today to Build God's Just Community

Jesus' Aunt and the Wife of Clopas: Two Unknown Women at the Cross (John 19: 25)
Few really know historically of the presence of Jesus' aunt and of Clopas' wife. Even fewer may care to know. Why, then, do we think they are important enough to lift up in this study, other than they were also members of the Movement of Jesus? First, every woman in that movement counted. Perhaps insignificant when considered individually, collectively these women contributed to announcing

the new day of God's open community. Their presence was so strikingly daring that the Gospel writers could not overlook their steadfast vigil at Jesus' crucifixion in Jerusalem. Secondly, the presence of two or more women together gives each one encouragement, strength, and support to engage in courageous acts. That is, when women are engaged faithfully in justice-seeking activity, having a sister in the struggle empowers each one to withstand hardship and danger that taking life-risking action brings. What one woman might have been reluctant to do, these women together were able to accomplish. Their witness made a powerfully profound statement to believers and non-believers alike. In an important sense, this illustrates for us the significance of women who may go unnoticed every day, but who are faithfully involved in important justice work. These women who stood by Jesus faithfully were rewarded with the earth-shattering news of Jesus' resurrection.

The Widow Who Struggled Until Justice Was Done (Luke 18:1-8).

This parable teaches us much about the power of society's most vulnerable—which may sound like a contradiction in terms. Usually the terms "vulnerable" or "weak" characterize those who have very little power or access to it. An amazing reversal happens in this parable, though. This frail woman, a widow, takes on the establishment, a corrupt judicial system that feels no responsibility for the poor, and secures for herself a blessing. Her willingness to risk provides a powerful example for women deemed "powerless" around the world. All women can learn from her bold daring and persistent trust that God's justice would prevail and so not accept things as they are.

1. As a total group, review the key Gospel stories for this activity: John 19: 25-27; Luke 18: 1-8, and the text pages 41-47. Looking closely at these accounts, consider the following:

- Identify the situation and the key people in each story.
- Describe the key issues in your own words.
- List the justice issues—factors that oppress or exclude.
- Identify the risks the women took.
- What were the results? What was gained?
- How was God's presence felt?

2. Now shift the focus to a current setting. Divide into two or more groups so that an equal number of groups will be assigned to the two Gospel stories in #1. Instruct each group to: a) identify contemporary issues and situations for each story (e.g., the women at the crucifixion could be two women present at a prison execution; the woman facing the unjust judge could be a current court scene about a woman's justice issue); b) rewrite each biblical story in contemporary language and setting. Use the detailed information in the study book and the information gleaned from the Scripture analysis in #1 to inform your work. Also use issues of *Response* and *New World Outlook* magazines for contemporary issues and examples.

An example of a justice issue and the response to it follows. Ask each group to present its contemporary "gospel story."

"A Rainbow of Hope for Abused Korean Women"
"The cozy two-story house in Queens, N.Y., could belong to any family, but this home is the Rainbow Center, a haven for Korean women in crisis. Most of the women at the Rainbow Center have been abandoned and/or abused by their American GI husbands. It was created in response to the tragic situation of one such woman.

"Chong France, abused and abandoned by her American GI husband in North Carolina, left her toddler alone in a hotel room to go to work. When the dresser that held the television fell on the child, there was no one present who could remove it. The child died of suffocation. Ms. France was convicted for the child's murder and sentenced to 20 years in prison. Only after persistent efforts to receive a pardon was she released.

"'The Rainbow Center is the only United Methodist ministry in the nation providing services for Korean-American women who are married to American GIs. It is also a place where lay people play a significant role providing leadership,' said Jung Soon Kim, executive staff for Korean-American Ministries, General Board of Global Ministries." (Excerpted from an article by Connie Walsh in *Response*, June 1999.)

3. Follow up the "gospel story" writing with these discussion questions: How can your unit of United Methodist Women expand its mission service? What population is underserved? How would you introduce that need to your unit? What needs are there locally?

Does your unit address those needs?

The Woman Who Doesn't Rest Until She Finds Something Precious She Has Lost (Luke 15: 8-10).
This parable draws the reader immediately into the economic situation of women. Her frantic efforts alert one to the desperate level of survival women endure to provide for their household—even half a cent matters. Her circumstance of economic hardship is not unknown to the women in factories in Haiti and the maquiladoras on the United States/Mexico border who work for less than one dollar a day. Unfortunately, similar situations exist in the United States in "sweatshops." We don't have to go as far as Haiti. We hear stories through our news media about Chinese immigrants who died from suffocation in storage containers while being smuggled into this country by ship. Of those who survive horrific voyages, many are forced to work under inhumane conditions that pay far below minimum wage in order to repay their passage, which may gouge them for $50,000 or more. This is another example of the need for solidarity with the marginalized, disempowered, and forsaken people in our world.

Optional Activity. Assign a group of volunteers to develop a skit that depicts an economic justice issue—a modern version of "The Woman Who Doesn't Rest Until She Finds Something Precious She Has Lost." Stage "A Day in the Life" of a woman working in a U.S.-based factory. She makes less than a dollar a day—perhaps as little as 20¢ or 30¢ —to feed her family. Develop the problems and tensions that emerge to sustain daily survival under such austere conditions. Work through the complex issues that impoverish her life. Go to a Web site and acquire necessary information: see General Board of Global Ministries pages: **http://gbgm-umc.org** and General Board of Church and Society: **http://umc-gbcs.org/**.

Activity 3:
The Woman Who Secretly Took a Miracle from Jesus (Mark 5: 21-43).

When Jesus makes known the action of this daring woman in a

crowded public street, he actively participates in challenging a system of rules and laws that otherwise would have been very difficult. Because of this woman's bold act, other marginalized women will also dare to transgress the patterns of society that marginalize them. The woman with an issue of blood dared to come out of her isolation and make her experience public as she sought healing. She literally stepped out in faith to confront her illness of 12 years. Jesus' action denied the power of fear and its ostracizing consequence. Through the centuries, women have gained courage to make public the convictions of their conscience to heal the deep wounds and injustices of religious and social systems. Joan of Arc, Anne Hutchinson, Sojourner Truth, and Elizabeth Cady Stanton defied opposing forces meant to silence them in their efforts to effect social transformation, especially on behalf of marginalized women. Drawing from the example of Jesus, then, means women moving out into the public arena in faith to build new ways of living and relating that challenge settled boundaries and barriers to the full inclusion of all people.

Questions for Discussion or Reflection: How do issues of women's health stigmatize women as "weak" or "undesirable" for certain functions? What do you feel about the ways that institutions have dealt with issues of women's health, such as the government, the religious sector, the medical community, etc.? Can you identify the "unclean" people today whom society still avoids touching? For example, would you touch, visit and/or assist a person who has AIDS or the HIV virus? Identify cultural, religious, and caste taboos in the U.S. and different parts of the world that restrictively label certain types of people (such as the "untouchables"–Dalits–of India). Cite Scripture references to support your position of advocacy. Consider these passages: Matthew 25: 32-46; Mark 5: 21-43; John 9: 1-11.

The Syrophoenician Woman Who Argues with Jesus (Mark 7:24-30; Matthew 15: 21-28).
She, a foreigner, urged by love for her daughter, waives the expectations of her own cultural norms and transgresses those of another culture to acquire what she seeks from Jesus: a healing for her daughter. This story teaches that women must do nothing less than

be daring and defiant when they know that what they seek is just and good. The Syrophoenecian woman's stubbornness performs a critical function in breaking down barriers to just treatment. Persistence, when born out of resistance, can change rules, conduct, customs, and attitudes that marginalize those who are foreign or immigrate to new areas, or are somehow "different." Through persistent acts, migrant and refugee peoples of our world find sanctuary for their woundedness from acts of war, economic exploitation, racial and gender issues.

Discussion Questions: Consider your local faith community. How does it welcome the stranger? Live with differences? For instance, most likely everyone won't have the same "difference," so how are differences of all kinds handled in your church?

Assignments for Session IV

- Assign Part II on "Women Teachers and Disciples," chapters 7-9 in the study text.
- Assign a volunteer to make a diagram of the lines of authority in your local United Methodist Church
- Assign a volunteer to report on the United Methodist resolution "The Status of Women,"in *The Book of Resolutions, 2000* (pages 459-464), originally adopted in 1992 by the General Conference. Make copies for class members.
- Give participants the list of words in the lefthand column of the "Word Study" on page 143 to be discussed in this session.
- Ask for a volunteer to paraphrase the John 4: 5-42 Scripture using a first-person account from a woman evangelist's point of view. (You might give her the name "Junia" since Paul called her an apostle in Romans 16: 7 or choose another name). Use the "I, Lydia" style to begin the story and go from there. Remember, it is not absolutely clear that the woman at the well was immoral. She could have been a victim of the system where a brother was expected to marry his deceased brother's wife. It is possible that after four deaths or divorces, the fifth man did not want to risk marriage but was willing to house her nevertheless. It could be argued that if she had been

immoral with five men, she already would have been stoned to death. Keep the paraphrase short. The text is very long but try to be concise.

- Ask for 2 or 3 volunteers to collect the names of women who have either influenced Christianity or started a religious movement. These names will be used in the Easter Banner Pageant.
- Ask for two volunteers to lead in song and dance for the Easter Banner Pageant.
- Ask a volunteer to bring an earthen pot to hold water. If practical, participants can bring water and containers or vessels to pour forth their water from different sources.

Closing Worship

Hymn: #593, "Here I Am, Lord," *The United Methodist Hymnal*, chorus only

Ritual of Solidarity: We Are God's Vessels.
Each person will bring to the worship table the object she or he has brought in. In a phrase, each person shall say what gift of self or of a biblical woman the object represents. It is each participant's offering to the building of the open or just community.

Closing Prayer
O God, we thank you for reaching beyond boundaries of gender, ethnicity, race, class, and so many others that we create. You invite all people to yourself. We ask that you strengthen, sustain, and empower us to reach out to others in the same welcoming and life-affirming way. In the name of Jesus, the Living Water. Amen.

—adapted from a prayer by April Yamasaki in *Remembering Lot's Wife and Other Unnamed Women of the Bible*. Copyright © 1991. Faith Quest, an imprint of Brethren Press, Elgin, IL. p. 98. Used by permission.

Hymn: #593, "Here I Am, Lord," *The United Methodist Hymnal*; repeat the chorus

Women Teachers and Disciples

Purpose: To proclaim the discipleship of women in the church

Objectives for This Session

- To challenge social and cultural assumptions of "male head-ship" as the order of creation in the church
- To examine lines of authority in the local church from a gender perspective
- To explain the transfer of power to male representatives in the faith community in contradiction to the Jesus tradition
- To foster solidarity with women in ministry
- To challenge fixed hierarchical divisions between ordained and lay ministries
- To focus on ways women can move from the margins of male-dominated structures to the center of church life

Preparing for the Session

- Gather supplies for the Easter Banner Pageant "In Memory of Her" on page 147. Set up small tables or parts of large tables as work stations for groups of four.
- Place water containers in a central place; provide a small paper cup for each participant.
- Provide *The United Methodist Hymnal* and extra Bibles.

Announcements

Opening Worship

Hymn: #405, "Seek Ye First," *The United Methodist Hymnal*

Scripture: John 4: 5-42, as interpreted by a class participant

Hymn: #405, "Seek Ye First," *The United Methodist Hymnal*

Introduction

We know that women figured considerably in Jesus' public ministry. This study lifts up Scripture passages that record the life stories and deeds of women which indicate unequivocally that the movement of Jesus, the Christ always included women disciples, apostles and missionaries. In the upper room prayer chamber, women, including Mary, the mother of Jesus (Acts 1:14), welcomed the visitation of the Holy Spirit with the hospitality of an open heart and greetings of praise. Likewise, women labored in the birthing of the house-church movement. Tirelessly, Priscilla and Lydia toiled with the Apostle Paul as co-laborers in organizing house-churches in their respective communities (Acts 2:46-47).

A "pecking-order" based on gender had no place in a movement that received the gifts and graces of men and women alike, and was characterized by the social reversal of expectations for poor and rich, Jew and Gentile, male and female. The last was assured the promise of being received, as well as the first. Women in the Movement of Jesus could fully embody the positions they believed themselves called to. Their true identity in God was affirmed. Indeed, Jesus' risk-taking deeds on behalf of women demonstrated his unquestioned commitment to women and his belief that they too embodied the image of God.

A WORD STUDY

This is an introduction to important terms found in the readings which reflect the New Testament social and cultural worldview during the house-church movement.

Term:

Match the word in the left column with the correct definition in the right column.

1. diakonos

   a. These rules were established by house-churches both to avoid chaos and to gain approval from Roman society, which often reinstated gender hierarchy.

2. community of equals

   b. Belief that males must own and rule a household. This was extended to rule of city, nation, and institutionalized religion.

3. house-church

   c. Values so accepted that they become the framework on which social structures are framed and maintained. When the values are questioned, defenders point to the institutions that might be threatened. When the institutions are threatened, they point to the values that are threatened.

4. domestic codes

   d. This community of believers participated in the Jesus movement through house-churches and public witness.

5. patriarchal household

   e. Acts 2: 43-47 provides an example where all was shared in common according to need.

6. institutionalization

   f. Early believers met in the homes of more prosperous members of the Jesus movement. Entire households were often converted such as "Cornelius and his household" (Acts 10: 1-48).

Key: 1. d., 2. e., 3. f., 4. a., 5. b., 6. c.

The Easter Story Revisited

Author Elsa Tamez notes that Mary Magdalene was a true apostle. Mary followed and became a part of the movement in Galilee. Later she was a grief-stricken witness to his death, but then she rejoiced in his Easter morning appearance as the Resurrected One.

All four Gospels mention Mary first in the list of witnesses to the resurrection of Jesus (Mark 16: 1-9; Matthew 28: 1; Luke 24: 10; John 20: 11-18). So why, as Tamez questions, is there such controversy in the early church around including Mary Magdalene's name as one of the first witnesses? The qualifications established by the early church to "qualify" as an apostle were: to bear witness to the resurrected Christ, and to have shared a privileged intimacy with Jesus while he walked the earth. Like Peter and Paul, Mary undoubtedly qualified. In the Orthodox tradition, Mary Magdalene is called "equal to the Apostles," a title unfamiliar to Protestants.

Then why and how was she marginalized among the apostles? According to scholar John Dominic Crossan, much of that historical controversy has to do with how "gender authority" was invested in our early and contemporary faith communities. Hierarchies based on the subordination of women developed in contradiction to the gender equality practiced in the Jesus tradition.

Learning Activities

1. "The Gospel of Mary." In the early Christian writing "The Gospel of Mary," read the section where Peter challenges the authority of Mary but the other disciples defend her. Discuss how this text might reflect the issues of Mary's leadership as well as the leadership of all women in the early church. (You can find "The Gospel of Mary" in Appendix C, p. 167, or at **gbgm-umc.org/umw/Bible/noncon.html**)

2. Probing Lines of Authority: A Gender Analysis. This activity will help us analyze some of the gender power arrangements in our own local churches. First draw a picture of how your church is run.

You can use symbols like circles, stick figures, etc. Think about how history would remember your local church or your congregation if it had died today. Write an epitaph that includes its treatment of women and girls.

Provide the chart or graph of the organization of a local United Methodist church. Without referring to it, ask participants as a group to graph the lines of authority in the leadership structure of the church giving attention to women's leadership. Ask them these questions: Where are the women in the structure? Do they hold important positions? Or are they consigned to subordinate roles? What about spiritual leadership? Do women in your local church give spiritual leadership without the "official" authority of position?*

Now ask participants to compare their group drawing with the official one. Are lines of leadership and authority the same? Where are the women? How do women exercise authority in your local church? Is it from the margin or the center? Was this always the case? When was there a change and how did it happen? Discuss for 10-15 minutes.

3. The House-Churches Practice Solidarity with Women in Ministry. The presence of Priscilla and Lydia, two working women and leaders of Christian communities, as recorded in Acts 16: 11-15, 40; 18: 1-4, 18-19, 24-28; Romans 16:3, invites us to regain an understanding of the church as a community of equals. Feminist biblical scholars Elsa Tamez and Elisabeth Schüssler Fiorenza argue that biblical and extra-biblical sources document the fact of women's gradual loss of voice and authority in the church starting

---

* In its 1999 quadrennial study of local church participation, the United Methodist Commission on the Status and Role of Women (COSROW) found that men still tended to be lay leaders instead of women, by a margin of 2 to 1. In the pulpit, 53 percent of the churches had had only one or no laywomen as preachers during the past year, and 77 percent had no clergywomen preaching. For lay liturgists, 35 percent used all or mostly males, while 39 percent used all or mostly females. Women also were least likely to participate in finance or missions committees or serve on the board of trustees. Twenty percent of the responding pastors said they didn't know which issues were important to the women in the local church. See the Web site: **http://www.umc.org/gcsrw**

at the end of the first century. The early church tradition that had formed around the discipleship of equals was phased out, with women ultimately being silenced. This occurred as Christians tried to gain acceptance in a Roman imperial society that practiced hierarchical modes of social relations. As Tamez rightly identifies, "The prophetic, radical critique voiced by Jesus and Paul in the face of any kind of oppression begins to be less apparent." (See page 99.) How can we, then, regain such "radicality" and act in solidarity with women? In the church, how can we promote partnership of male and female leadership? Lastly, how must women work to prevent titles of lay and ordained from dividing our mutual strength and common cause?

a. With the help of the leader, identify 4 or 5 women in diverse ministries. Consider women who: minister to women in prison; minister to congregations; run battered women's shelters; run community centers; are deaconesses, etc. Invite them to a roundtable discussion sponsored by your unit or a class group, and ask them to speak specifically about their experience in ministry. Broadly define women in ministry, whether ordained or lay. Also seek out those who serve in non-traditional settings. Explore what it means to choose ordination and ministry as a layperson.

b. Another option is to visit 4 or 5 women in the context of their ministry and talk with them there. Similar questions as the above apply. Get a sense of their routine and their struggle. What do they foresee for the future of women's ministry within the institutional church and beyond its walls?

4. Away from the Margins. Pass out the resolution copied from *The Book of Resolutions, 2000* on pages 459-464. "The Status of Women" resolution rejects institutionalized male power structures in the church. What woman in the Christian church has not heard the uncritical application of certain domestic codes sifted from the letters attributed to Paul (Colossians 3: 17-19 and Ephesians 5: 21f) as well as 1 Peter 2: 13? Or what woman is unfamiliar with the injunction for women to be silent in church? Another popular proscription is that women should not usurp/exert authority over men (1 Timothy 2: 11-13). These New Testament injunctions have troubled biblical scholars. Historically, the Church has accepted these texts as normative. Saddled with the imposed "burden" of gender, far too many women have had to lead from the margins rather than the center. The United Methodist Church, in a bold act of solidarity with women, adopted a resolution in 1992, 1996, and 2000 that rejects every intent to confine women to the margins of the church or the periphery of society. Ask the person who volunteered to highlight contents of this resolution. Then as a total group or in small groups discuss the following questions: How does this re-envisioning of women's empowerment facilitate moving women away from the margins in the church and in society? How is institutional violence against women revealed? Why and how so? List ways of presenting this resolution in the local church and embodying it in practice and policies.

5. In Memory of Her: A Pageant. On one occasion, rebuking his disciples for begrudging a selfless act of anointing by an unnamed woman whom many considered a known prostitute, Jesus says, "Let her alone, why do you trouble her?" In the end she receives an astonishing promise from him, words entrusted with deep possibilities for women: "Truly I tell you, wherever the good news is proclaimed in the whole world, what she has done will be told in remembrance of her." (Mark 14: 9). His words echo down through the centuries as a breath of hope for women. It breathes new life into the witness of women, on behalf of women.

Celebrating Our Foremothers in Faith
Break up into groups of two, especially for those interested in the same woman. Groups of four could share a small work station. Each work area might include women's folk art materials such as ribbons, bows, buttons, yarn, floral petals, cloth, etc. to create a banner depicting a woman's name and contribution. Have a dancer and song leader in place to lead off the parade of banners. Make it festive, inaugural. Have the group sing the Spiritual chorus "Oh Mary don't ya weep." Each time instead of singing "Pharaoh's army got drowned" sing the woman's name and "she was called." For example, "Oh Mary, don't ya weep don't ya mourn, Annie Norton was called, Oh Mary, don't ya weep." Then hum the same tune as a woman's story is read while her banner is front and center. (This brief presentation could also be used during a service for a United

Methodist Women's Sunday.) Before you begin, have the group identify two or three other United Methodist women and write a paragraph about them. Lift up some of our unsung United Methodist foremothers. Such names could include:

Isabella Thoburn, 1840-1901, Woman's Foreign Missionary Society, Methodist Episcopal Church

Isabella Thoburn became the first missionary of the Woman's Foreign Missionary Society. Miss Thoburn arrived in India on January 7, 1870, went to Lucknow and opened her school on April 18 of the same year, with six girls enrolled. Out of that little school came the first Christian college for women in Asia.

Annie Pascoe Norton, M.D., 1846-1926, Woman's Foreign Missionary Society, Methodist Episcopal Church

At age 53, Annie Pascoe Norton was licensed to practice medicine and surgery in New York and Ohio. She then became a missionary and was sent by the Methodist Episcopal Church to the Philippine Islands, along with three other women, Julia Wisner, Mary Cody, and Cornelia Moots. She was the first medical missionary sent to the Philippines and in 1905 received her license to practice medicine there. Living in the Philippines for 26 years, she started the first Woman's Christian Temperance Union there.

Isabelle Harris Bennett, 1852-1922, Woman's Home Missionary Society, Woman's Missionary Council, Methodist Episcopal Church, South.

In 1886, Belle Bennett felt that God was calling her for a specific service through the woman's missionary work of her church. Until her death, she worked unceasingly in the church, becoming one of its most outstanding leaders. Because of her special concern for a training school for women Christian workers, she was commissioned by the Woman's Foreign Missionary Society, along with Maria Wightman, to raise funds for building the Scarritt Bible and Training School in Kansas City, Missouri, later renamed Scarritt College. Belle Bennett was president of the Woman's

Board of Home Missions from 1896 to 1910, and president of the Woman's Missionary Council from 1910 to 1922.

Minerva Strawman Spreng 1854-1924, Woman's Missionary Society, Evangelical Association

Miss Strawman and the women of the Lindsey, Ohio, church organized the first Woman's Society in the Evangelical Association in 1880. Four years later, Mrs. Minerva Strawman Spreng was elected third vice-president of the Woman's Missionary Society of the Evangelical Association. From 1892 to 1922, she was its president and then president of the Women's Missionary Society of the Evangelical Church from 1922 to 1924, a total of 32 years.

[The bios above are excerpted from *They Went Out Not Knowing: 100 Women in Mission, An Encyclopedia of 100 Women in Mission*, Women's Division, General Board of Global Ministries, The United Methodist Church, 1982.]

Pioneer Marjorie Matthews 'knew the call'

"When Marjorie Matthews became a United Methodist bishop at age 64, newspapers across the country announced the news with headlines such as 'The bishop is a woman.' The year was 1980, and Matthews was the first woman to become a bishop in The United Methodist Church. Though a pioneer, she served only one term as bishop, leading the Wisconsin Area for four years before retiring in 1984. She died in 1986." By Sharon Fulmer (see Appendix A on page 165.)

Assignments for Session V

1. Ask one or two participants to read excerpts from early Methodist women's history. Sources could include *Women in New Worlds: Historical Perspectives on the Wesleyan Tradition*, eds. Hillah F. Thomas & Rosemary Skinner Keller; *Spirituality and Social Responsibility*, ed. Rosemary Keller; *Grace Sufficient: A History of Women in American Methodism 1760-1939*. They will contribute to Session V.

2. Ask for volunteers to visit the Women's Division Web site at **http://gbgm-umc.org/UMW** and the UM General Commission on Archives and History web site: **http://gcah.org/women_ministry.htm** under "Resources" for historical information to use in the activity on page 155.
3. Assign the excerpt from *The Beijing Declaration and Platform for Action, Fourth World Conference on Women*, Beijing, China, 4-15 September 1995 on pages 159-60. Access the Web site for the entire document: **http://un.org/womenwatch/daw/beijing/platform**
4. Ask for four volunteers to lead worship for the next session. They will do a choral presentation, reading simultaneously the four Gospel versions of Jesus' death and resurrection. Use different languages if possible. This choral Scripture reading is available from the Women's Division Web site: **http://gbgm-umc.org/umw/jesusandwomen/**

Closing Worship

Chorus: #641, "Fill My Cup, Lord," *The United Methodist Hymnal*

Sing once and hum while you invite the participants to share water from their homes—wherever they "draw water." Combine the waters and then pour them into small cups for each person. Have the cups ready but do not drink yet.

All: We come to you, O Christ, asking for living water, and like the woman at the well, we are sometimes shocked when you speak to us. You know us and know our lives. We must tell the world!

Hymn: #427, "Where Cross the Crowded Ways of Life," *The United Methodist Hymnal*, verse 1

Unison Response: We hear the cry of race and clan. We also hear the noise which silences women. Women have been called cackling hens when talking together. Women have been shoved aside when leaders are needed. We hear your voice, O

Son of Man, and know that you were the son of a woman and a friend of many women.

Hymn: #427, verse 3

Unison Response: We seek songs that bring in the lives of women and find a few verses. When we find them, they often refer to Eve's curse, when in fact, Eve was never cursed; she was given the trappings of humanity like clothing and birthing.

Hymn: #427, verse 4

Unison Response: We know the cup of water was given to a woman. Once again, even in a powerful song about justice and grace, the woman disappears. Her bold questions and sudden evangelistic announcement get lost. This day we remember her and the living water which she announced to her people.

Hymn: #427, verse 5

Unison Response: We want to walk where your feet have walked but we are so rarely reminded that you walked with women on hillsides, in homes, in the streets and in desert towns. And they walked with you through the hours of your crucifixion and the sunrise of your resurrection.

Chorus: #647, "Fill My Cup, Lord"

As you sing, invite the participants to come forth to drink from the living waters that Christ offers. Come as women with histories, memories, and stories to tell to the nations.

All: O God, you have known us and seen us for who we are, humble women, bold women, condemned women, lauded women. We are no more and no less than children of the most high. Grant us the wisdom to use the gifts you offer with courage and with confidence. AMEN! WE GO FORTH!

Session V :

A Resurrection Future for United Methodist Women

Purpose: To affirm the commitment and mission of United Methodist Women to women's spiritual and social empowerment all over the world

Objectives for This Session
- To become familiar with the institutional history of United Methodist Women
- To explore possibilities for *The Beijing Declaration and The Platform for Action* in lay terms for local United Methodist churches
- To explore strategies for a Resurrection Future for United Methodist Women

Preparing for the Session
- Make copies of the diagram of "United Methodist Women Yesterday, Today and Tomorrow" from the book *They Went Out Not Knowing: 100 Women in Mission, An Encyclopedia of 100 Women in Mission*, Women's Division, General Board of Global Ministries, The United Methodist Church, pp. 52-53 (#3806, $3.25). Make 3 sets of copies, enough for each participant to have one. In each set, block out different facts to create a fill-in-the-blank exercise (use "post-its" for temporary coverup).

- Provide copies of a recent *Report of the Women's Division* (see the current Service Center Catalog).
- Prepare copies of *The Beijing Declaration and The Platform for Action* available from **http://www.un.org/womenwatch/daw/ beijing/platform/** if you use more than the excerpt on pages 159-60.
- Print and post examples of "Mission Stories" from the General Board of Global Ministries Web site: **http://gbgm-umc.org/** or from issues of *Response* or *New World Outlook*.
- Post newsprint for large group discussion.
- Supply sheets of construction paper and other supplies for activity 5.
- Provide *The United Methodist Hymnal*.
- Arrange for VCR, monitor, and the UMW video *Theressa Hoover: A Woman with Purpose*. Order #3004, $15.00 from the Service Center. Preview the video before the session.

Announcements

Opening Worship

Hymn:
Were you there when they crucified my Lord?
Were you there when they crucified my Lord?
Oh, sometimes it causes me to tremble, tremble, tremble.
Were you there when they crucified my Lord?

Scripture Reading: Choral Reading from the Four Gospels (from the Web site, **http://gbgm-umc.org/umw/jesusandwomen**)

Hymn:
She was there when he rose up from the grave!
She was there when he rose up from the grave!
Oh, sometimes it cause me to tremble, tremble, tremble.
She was there when he rose up from the grave!

Introduction

United Methodist Women are resurrection women. Like the first disciples of Jesus, although faced with obstacles of class, race, gender and more, we have felt called to a new way of living together, sharing, organizing, celebrating, and struggling. We are called to resurrection hope that can transform social order. United Methodist Women have responded to the resurrection mandate "Go, tell my disciples" through acts of love and solidarity that reach around the globe. Our advocacy on behalf of the oppressed and the dispossessed spans more than a century of mission. This rich legacy from the past continues. Activities in recent years include work to: ban landmines; stop sweatshop abuses and child labor; reduce dioxin contamination; challenge strawberry growers who violate workers' rights; and implement the United Nations Universal Declaration of Human Rights.

At the 2000 General Conference, the Women's Division proposed several resolutions that were adopted as United Methodist Church policy. One decried the recruitment and training of children as soldiers, and another resolution condemned the targeting of children, especially girls, for sexual abuse and gender-based violence. Also adopted is a resolution calling for the church to monitor and advocate against hate crimes that target people of color, gay men and lesbians, religious minorities, and women.

Learning Activities

1. UMW History Inventory. How much United Methodist Women's history do you know? When participants come into the class, ask them to assemble in three groups. Hand out three sets of altered diagrams of "United Methodist Women Yesterday, Today and Tomorrow." For five minutes work in small groups. Then have the people from each group work with others if there are any incomplete facts. Share discoveries as a total group.

2. United Methodist Women's History: Through Her Eyes. Twenty-nine years ago the Women's Society of Christian Service and the Wesleyan Service Guild came together to create one organization. These two organizations represented the women's organizations of the Evangelical United Brethren and the Methodist Churches that had united just four years previously. The legacy from our predecessor organizations dates back to 1869 when the Woman's Foreign Missionary Society was formed. The diagram activity above was an introduction to the organizational history of United Methodist Women. Go over the diagram with the class and fill in the gaps. Solicit answers and comments from the class.

3. Our lives. Have each participant write a brief autobiography related to her or his work with United Methodist Women. You may want to create a booklet to be distributed.

4. As an activity outside of class, send class participants to the United Methodist Women's conference archives or Web site to identify primary sources, such as minutes, letters, diaries, journals, autobiographies, etc., written by women and women's organizations now part of United Methodist Women. Excerpt information from the sources to provide the class with an experiential sense of United Methodist Women's history. Also see Women's Division history at the Web site: **http://gbgm-umc.org/UMW**, and the CD-ROM: *Ten Best Books on the History of United Methodist Women* (#2829, $40).

5. Divide the class in small groups and give them each biographies of the following women. Select a symbol for each woman and draw it on an 8 1/2" x 5 1/2" piece of construction paper. Have class members also make a symbol from their own autobiographies. Using either masking tape on paper or walls, or a large piece of cloth sprayed with adhesive (find in office, department, or craft stores), make a paper quilt out of all the symbols. Take time to say the name and one phrase about the person (perhaps in epitaph form such as "Justina Showers was a leader in young women's work and was the first president of the EUB women's organization.")

6. Show the video *Theressa Hoover: A Woman with PURPOSE.* Order #3004, $15.00 from the Service Center (See page 182 for ordering information). Or research some of these important figures in United Methodist Women's history on the Women's Division Web site or the CD-ROM *Ten Best Books on the History of United Methodist Women* (see 5 above):

Susan M. Bauernfeind, *1870-1945, Woman's Missionary Society, Evangelical Association*

One of the first two women missionaries sent to Japan by the Woman's Missionary Society of the Evangelical Association, Susan M. Bauernfeind landed in Japan on October 10, 1900, and served there faithfully for 43 years. Her achievements included the beginning of a social center in Japan's largest spinning factory in 1902, the establishment in 1904 of the Tokyo Bible School, the founding of the Aisenryo Orphanage for homeless girls, and the organization of the Japan Branch of the Woman's Missionary Society in 1918. A church in Japan was named in her honor.

Elida García de Falcón, *1879-1968, Woman's Society of Christian Service, The Methodist Church*

Elida García de Falcón attended what is now Southwest Texas State University, taught in Texas public schools, was a writer and poet, and contributed to many of the Spanish newspapers published in Texas. From 1943 to 1964 Mrs. Falcón translated the Program Book into Spanish for the Woman's Division of Christian Service. Along with her daughter, Clotilde Falcón Náñez, she spent 26 consecutive years translating. Mrs. Falcón also translated many of the hymns in the *Himnario Metodista*, the official hymnal of Hispanic Methodism in the United States.

Martha Ann Drummer, *(circa) 1880-1937, Woman's Foreign Missionary Society, Methodist Episcopal Church*

Martha Ann Drummer received a tuition scholarship to Clark College in Atlanta, and while at Clark decided to be a missionary. Following graduation in 1901, she entered the Northeastern Deaconess Training School in Boston to major in nursing, and graduated in 1904. She was the second black missionary accepted for service by the Woman's Foreign Missionary Society. She sailed for Quessua, Angola, in 1906, after serving briefly with the Woman's Home Missionary Society. She served sixteen years in Angola and Portuguese West Africa.

Justina Lorenz Showers, *1885-1985, Women's Missionary Association, United Brethren Church*
Justina Lorenz Showers was elected the first secretary of Young Women's Work of the Women's Missionary Association of the United Brethren Church, after graduation from Bryn Mawr College in Pennsylvania. This organization was the forerunner of the Otterbein Guild for girls. She was on the Association's Board of Trustees for twenty-five years, and served as its president from 1941 to 1946. When the Evangelical and United Brethren Churches united to become the Evangelical United Brethren Church, she was elected the first president of the Women's Society of World Service and served from 1947 to 1954.

Louise Johanna Nienas Busacca, *1888-1981, Woman's Missionary Society, Evangelical Church*
Louise Johanna Nienas moved with her family to Wisconsin, where she received a degree in elementary education. Working as a public school teacher in Racine, Wisconsin, she volunteered as a teacher in the nearby Sunday School of the Italian Mission. She married the student pastor of the church, and together they helped this new congregation grow in numbers and in depth of faith. Commissioned by the Evangelical Church, the Busaccas were a part of their church's response to the early twentieth-century influx of Italian immigrants in the highly industrialized cities of Milwaukee, Racine, and Kenosha, Wisconsin. Louise and her husband moved to Kenosha in 1922 to open a new mission for Italian immigrants.

May C. Chun, *1923- , Woman's Society of Christian Service, The Methodist Church*
May Chun is a woman of many "firsts." She was born the first daughter in a Chinese family already honored by a son. She was the first woman to be Assistant Superintendent of Education and state librarian in the Hawaii State Department of Education. Although active as a leader throughout her journey of faith, May's almost full-time voluntarism in the church began in 1978 after retirement. In 1981, she became the first ethnic minority president of United Methodist Women of the Pacific and Southwest Conference. Her willingness to pioneer, risk and act as a change agent has made her a role model among Asian and other ethnic minority women. In

1984, she was presented the Bishop Gerald H. Kennedy Lay Woman of the Year Award by the then Pacific and Southwest Conference.

Mary E. Sato Takamine, *1916-1976, Woman's Society of Christian Service, The Methodist Church*
Mary Sato Takamine attributed her initial commitment to the church to her mother, an immigrant from Japan, who accepted Christianity and strove to be a Christian witness. Always interested in helping youth, she started Girl Scout troops in inner city churches. Mary was church secretary for Simpson United Methodist Church, a Japanese church in Denver, Colorado. As Sunday School superintendent, she made church come alive for many youth. She recognized the importance of the ethnic church and went to district meetings to raise the church's consciousness on this issue. Very involved in the Women's Society of Christian Service, and later United Methodist Women, she was elected to the Women's Division in 1976, a highlight of her life. She died shortly after the first Division meeting.

> Excerpted from *They Went Out Not Knowing: 100 Women in Mission. An Encyclopedia of 100 Women in Mission*, Women's Division, General Board of Global Ministries, The United Methodist Church (#3806, $3.25)

7. United Methodist Women in Action. The Women's Division works cooperatively to address global women's issues through various institutions such as the United Nations, the World Council of Churches (WCC), UniFem, and other non-governmental organizations. The World Council of Churches has declared a "Decade Against All Forms of Violence" which it officially launched on February 4, 2001. It will run until 2010 and coincides with the United Nations' "Decade for a Culture of Peace and Nonviolence for the Children of the World."

Women from around the world developed *The Beijing Declaration and Platform for Action*. The following text is the introduction to the document.

> The Platform for Action is a powerful agenda for the empowerment of women. It calls for the integration of gender perspectives in all policies and programs. It focuses on concrete

measures to address the critical areas of concern worldwide. The platform is a call for concrete action to make a difference:[1]

Action to protect and promote the human rights of women and the girl child as an integral part of universal human rights;

Action to eradicate the persistent and increasing burden of poverty on women;

Action to remove the obstacles to women's full participation in public life and decision-making, at all levels—including the family;

Action to eliminate all forms of violence against women;

Action to ensure equal access for girl children and women to education and health services;

Action to promote economic autonomy for women, and ensure their access to productive resources; and

Action to encourage an equitable sharing of family responsibilities.

Divide the class into three or four small groups. Estimate the number according to the size of the class. Assign each group task A, B or C below.

A. *The Beijing Declaration and Platform for Action* is designed for action on a local level with global possibilities. What does this mean? In other words, how does a grassroots congregation effect changes that have global implications? What strategies can the group suggest?

---

1. *The Beijing Declaration and The Platform for Action: Fourth World Conference on Women*, Beijing, China, 4-15 September 1995 (New York Department of Public Information: United Nations, 1996), 2-3.

B. Using *The Beijing Declaration and Platform for Action* booklet or excerpts from the Web site, select sections that the group can agree upon for potential worship experiences. Draw themes and information from the literature provided. Create rituals and litanies that emphasize embodiment. Move the discussion into how the information rendered in the booklet can be creatively embodied for integration into the worship life of the community.

C. Review *The Beijing Declaration and Platform for Action* for use in a series of Bible studies for your local church community. Consider what sections could be adapted for the series. Think about how you could take this Bible study back to your church and partner with other committees, such as the social justice ministry, Christian education committee, international affairs, missions, etc. Through this activity, the church community could be made more aware of international concerns related to women.

8. Strategies for a Resurrection Future. Review the types of work the Women's Division supports and the "Mission Stories." Invite a speaker from the Women's Division (call 1-212-870-3845). Discuss ways in which the local unit can support and encourage the work of the organization. Plan a trip to the offices in New York or in the regions as a women's group; bring a youth group along. Bring back the work of the Division to the local unit.

Closing Worship

A Celebration of 29 Years of Service to Christ and God's People

Hymn: #114, "Many Gifts, One Spirit," *The United Methodist Hymnal*, verses 1 and 2

Scripture: 1 Corinthians 13: 1-13

Reading (*in unison*): The PURPOSE of United Methodist Women

The organized unit of United Methodist Women shall be a community of women whose PURPOSE is to know God and to experience freedom as whole persons through Jesus Christ; to develop a creative supportive fellowship; and to expand concepts of mission through participation in the global ministries of the church.

Hymn: #114, verse 3

Affirmation of Peace and Justice

I believe in God, who is love, who created all people in God's own image, and who said of all creation that it is very good.

I believe in Jesus Christ, who came to heal us, and to free us from all forms of oppression.

I believe in the Spirit of God, who works in and through all who are turned towards the truth.

I believe in the community of faith, which is called to be at the service of all people.

I believe in God's promise to finally destroy the power of sin and to establish justice and peace for all humankind.

I do not believe in the right of the strongest or in the force of arms, or in the power of oppression.

I believe in human rights, and in the solidarity of all people.

I do not believe in racism, in the power that comes from wealth and privilege, or in any established order that enslaves.

I believe that all people, female and male, are equally human, and that order based on violence and injustice is not order.

I believe that war and hunger are not inevitable and that peace is possible.

I do not believe that suffering need be in vain, that death is the end, that the disfigurement of our world is what God intended.

I dare to believe, always and in spite of everything, in God's power to transform and change, bringing about the promise of a new heaven and a new earth where justice and peace will flourish.

—Adapted from a creed from Indonesia, which appeared in *Women in a Changing World*, World Council of Churches, June 1988. Reprinted in Worldview 10, no. 1(1991): 25. From *Women in a Changing World*, no. 26, June 1988, Geneva. Used by permission.

Closing Blessing (*in unison*):

We celebrate the many gifts and one Spirit which have made United Methodist Women possible. We celebrate that alone we are candles in the wind but together we let our light so shine before the world that the light cannot be put out. We go forth to be the people of God in the midst of God's world. Amen.

Appendices

APPENDIX A

Maud Keister Jensen: First woman to receive full clergy rights in the Methodist Church

Maud Keister Jensen, 94, the first woman to receive full clergy rights as an ordained pastor in the Methodist Church, died Oct. 12 in Madison, NJ.

Jensen, a long-time missionary to Korea, was admitted to the Central Pennsylvania Annual Conference "on trial" on May 18, 1956, which made her eligible to become a full member after two years.

The 1956 General Conference had approved full clergy rights for qualified women pastors only a short time before Jensen was admitted in Central Pennsylvania. Previously, women could be ordained as "local preachers" and appointed as "supply preachers" but were not permitted to be voting members of an annual conference and could not be assured of pastoral assignments.

In fact, Jensen had been ordained deacon by the Central Pennsylvania Conference in 1948 and ordained elder in 1952, so in 1956 the conference admitted her on the usual two-year trial basis. The action was taken in absentia because Jensen was serving as a missionary in Korea at the time.

Pioneer Marjorie Matthews 'knew the call'

Dec. 5, 2000 by Sharon Fulmer

ROCHESTER, N.Y. (UMNS) -- When Marjorie Matthews became a United Methodist bishop at age 64, newspapers across the country announced the news with headlines like, "The bishop is a woman." The year was 1980, and Matthews was the first woman to become a bishop in The United Methodist Church. Though a pioneer, she served only one term as bishop, leading the Wisconsin Area for four years before retiring in 1984. She died in 1986.

Men and women gathered on Nov. 16 to celebrate the 20th

anniversary of Matthews' election as bishop and to reflect on the role that women play in the church today. The event was held at Colgate Rochester Divinity School in Rochester, N.Y., where Matthews graduated in 1970.

Bishop Violet Fisher, who was elected in July and appointed to the New York West Area, noted that her own journey had taken "some of the twists and turns" that Matthews faced.

"I was told again and again, 'you can't do that,'" Fisher said. "I say, 'Be persistent, trust the spirit.'"

Fisher recalled some of the obstacles that she had to overcome in her career and that injustices still exist today. But, she said, "I knew I was called to this. Our sister knew the call."

Matthews was born in Michigan, one of six children of a barrel maker. In a presentation on Matthews' life, the Rev. Kathy Sage, a staff member at the divinity school, said the late bishop was "a very private person."

While serving her four-year term in Wisconsin, Matthews strived to "accustom people to the idea that either a man or a woman can be a bishop." Although most accepted and supported her, Matthews told the *New York Times* in an interview that the opposition she faced from churches sometimes surprised her. "They would tell people in my church they were going to hell for having a woman minister."

APPENDIX B

2000 General Conference: Women gain in leadership roles, but lose ground on path to full/equal participation

At the 1996 General Conference we celebrated the 40th anniversary of the ordination of women. That milestone symbolizes the significant progress The United Methodist Church has made toward bringing about the full and equal participation of women in the church. At the close of the 2000 General Conference, which met May 2-12 in Cleveland, we can celebrate the leadership provided by women as delegates, officers of legislative committees and subcommittees, worship leaders, bishops, executives of general agencies, and many other roles.

Yet any celebration of the 2000 General Conference must be

tempered with the recognition that women stand to lose some of our hard-won ground along our journey toward full and equal participation. The decision to change the formula for determining General Conference representation threatens to reduce the proportion of women elected as delegates to the next quadrennial meeting. (Of the 830 U.S. delegates, 324, or 39%, were women. Of the 992 total delegates, 359, or 36%, were women.)

APPENDIX C

Excerpts from the Gospel of Mary

Introduction: The Gospel of Mary is a noncanonical or outside book of Gnostic origin in the first or second century. Material in brackets are editorial additions and comments. The Coptic papyrus, from which the first six pages have been lost, begins in the middle of this gospel.

Existing Text:

"...will, then, matter be saved or not?"

The Savior said, "All natures, all formed things, all creatures exist in and with one another and will again be resolved into their own roots, because the nature of matter is dissolved into the roots of its nature alone. He who has ears to hear, let him hear." [cf. Matt. 11: 15, etc.].

Peter said to him, "Since you have now explained all things to us, tell us this: what is the sin of the world?" [cf. John 1: 29]. The Savior said, "Sin as such does not exist, but you make sin when you do what is of the nature of fornication, which is called 'sin.' For this reason the Good came into your midst, to the essence of each nature, to restore it to its root." He went on to say, "For this reason you come into existence and die [...] whoever knows may know [...] a suffering which has nothing like itself, which has arisen out of what is contrary to nature. Then there arises a disturbance in the whole body. For this reason I said to you, Be of good courage [cf.

Matt. 28:9], and if you are discouraged, still take courage over against the various forms of nature. He who has ears to hear, let him hear." When the Blessed One said this, he greeted all of them, saying "Peace be with you [cf. John 14:27]. Receive my peace for yourselves. Take heed lest anyone lead you astray with the words, 'Lo, here!' or 'Lo, there!' [cf. Matt. 24:5, 23; Luke 17:21] for the Son of Man is within you [cf. Luke 17:21]. Follow him; those who seek him will find him [cf. Matt. 7:7]. Go, therefore, and preach the Gospel of the Kingdom [cf. Matt. 4:23; 9:15; Mark 16:15]. I have left no commandment but what I have commanded you, and I have given you no law, as the lawgiver did, lest you be bound by it."

They grieved and mourned greatly, saying, "How shall we go to the Gentiles and preach the Gospel of the Kingdom of the Son of Man? If even he was not spared, how shall we be spared?"

Then Mary stood up and greeted all of them and said to her brethren, "Do not mourn or grieve or be irresolute, for his grace will be with you all and will defend you. Let us rather praise his greatness, for he prepared us and made us into men." When Mary said this, their hearts changed for the better, and they began to discuss the words of the [Savior].

Peter said to Mary, "Sister, we know that the Savior loved you more than other women [cf. John 11:5, Luke 10:38-42]. Tell us the words of the Savior which you have in mind since you know them; and we do not, nor have we heard of them."

Mary answered and said, "What is hidden from you I will impart to you." And she began to say the following words to them. "I," she said, "I saw the Lord in a vision and I said to him, 'Lord, I saw you today in a vision.' He answered and said to me, 'Blessed are you, since you did not waver at the sight of me. For where the mind is, there is your countenance' [cf. Matt. 6:21]. I said to him, 'Lord, the mind which sees the vision, does it see it through the soul or through the spirit?' The Savior answered and said, 'It sees neither through the soul nor through the spirit, but the mind, which is between the two, which sees the vision, and it is...'"

"...and Desire said, 'I did not see you descend; but now I see you rising. Why do you speak falsely, when you belong to me?' The soul answered and said, 'I saw you, but you did not see me or recognize me; I served you as a garment and you did not recognize me.' After it had said this, it went joyfully and gladly away. Again it came to the third power, Ignorance. This power questioned the soul: 'Whither are you going? You were bound in wickedness, you were bound indeed. Judge not' [cf. Matt. 7:1]. And the soul said, 'Why do you judge me, when I judged not? I was bound, though I did not bind. I was not recognized, but I recognized that all will go free, things both earthly and heavenly.' After the soul had left the third power behind, it rose upward, and saw the fourth power, which had seven forms. The first form is darkness, the second desire, the third ignorance, the fourth the arousing of death, the fifth is the kingdom of the flesh, the sixth is the wisdom of the folly of the flesh, the seventh is wrathful wisdom. These are the seven participants in wrath. They ask the soul, 'Whence do you come, killer of men, or where are you going, conqueror of space?' The soul answered and said, 'What seizes me is killed; what turns me about is overcome; my desire has come to an end and ignorance is dead. In a world I was saved from a world, and in a "type," from a higher "type" and from the fetter of the impotence of knowledge, the existence of which is temporal. From this time I will reach rest in the time of the moment of the Aeon in silence.'"

When Mary had said this, she was silent, since the Savior had spoken thus far with her. But Andrew answered and said to the brethren, 'Say what you think concerning what she said. For I do not believe that the Savior said this. For certainly these teachings are of other ideas."

Peter also opposed her in regard to these matters and asked them about the Savior. "Did he then speak secretly with a woman [cf. John 4:27], in preference to us, and not openly? Are we to turn back and all listen to her? Did he prefer her to us?"

Then Mary grieved and said to Peter, "My brother Peter, what do you think? Do you think that I thought this up myself in my heart or that I am lying concerning the Savior?"

Levi answered and said to Peter, "Peter, you are always irate. Now I see that you are contending against the woman like the adversaries. But if the Savior made her worthy, who are you to reject her? Surely the Savior knew her very well [cf. Luke 10:38- 42]. For this reason he loved her more than us [cf. John 11:5]. And we should rather be ashamed and put on the Perfect Man, to form us [?] as he commanded us, and proclaim the gospel, without publishing a further commandment or a further law than the one which the Savior spoke." When Levi had said this, they began to go out in order to proclaim him and preach him.

Glossary

Anachronism: something that is out of its time, usually an idea or object that is projected into a time during which it did not exist.

Androcentric: From androcentrism. Term from the Greek that signifies the centrality of the male (andro-), or that everything revolves around men.

Apocryphal: Of unknown or hidden origin; refers to books that are not included in the Bible because church tradition considers them not to be inspired.

B.C.E.: Before the Common Era, or before the Christian era; more inclusive than B.C.

C.E.: Common Era; or Christian era; a more inclusive term than A.D. (Anno Domini).

Diaspora: the Jewish communities living dispersed outside Palestine, mostly in large cities such as Alexandria, Corinth, and Rome.

Enigma: a mystery or riddle; something that is difficult to explain.

Epiphany: a manifestation of the presence of God that may occur by means of angels or messengers. Also used to refer to the appearance of Christ after the resurrection. (*The* Epiphany, however, is the feast day on which church tradition celebrates the coming of the Magi to the infant Jesus, or the manifestation of

Christ's glory to the nations of the world.)

God-fearer: a Gentile converted to Judaism.

Hellenism: adoption of Greek customs and language in the non-Greek areas conquered by Alexander the Great in the 4th century B.C.E. Hellenistic cities included Alexandria in Egypt and Antioch in Syria, both of which became centers of Christian activity after the New Testament period.

Hierarchical: ordering authority according to rank of power or prestige; a top-down structure.

Ideology: a system of ideas that explains and justifies a social, political, economic, and cultural program.

Interpolation: a fragment of a text that has been inserted by another hand into an original in order to embellish or explain it.

Marginalized: completely or mostly left out of the predominant economic and cultural power structure.

Midrash: a method of interpreting Scripture by creating stories that enhance or explain a text by developing character or plot elements or events that occur off-stage or in between scenes.

Patriarchal: from patriarchy: a system of social, economic, political and legal relationships in which the father is the head of the family and the entire household depends on him. In this system the condition of women is one of submission. Most well-known ancient societies were strongly patriarchal.

Sanhedrin: the council of Jewish elders in Jerusalem who heard and judged matters relating to Jewish law within the Jewish community (they had no jurisdiction over the Romans), before 70 C.E.

Synoptic: a label given to the first three Gospels (Matthew, Mark and Luke) which share a similar style and outlook; from the Greek meaning "with one eye."

Selected Bibliography

Batista, Esperanza. *La mujer en la iglesia primitiva*. Estella, Spain: Verbo Divino, 1993.

Carlisle, Thomas John. *Beginning with Mary: Women of the Gospels in Portrait*. Grand Rapids, Mich.: Wm. B. Eerdmans, 1986.

*Clarkson, J. Shannon. *Conflict and Community in the Corinthian Church*. New York: General Board of Global Ministries, The United Methodist Church, 2000 (#2869, $4.50)

Coffey, Kathy. *Hidden Women of the Gospels*. New York: The Crossroad Publishing Co., 1998.

*DeBoer, Esther. *Mary Magdalene: Beyond the Myth*. Valley Forge, Penn.: Trinity Press International, 1997. (#3145, $15.00)

Foulkes, Irene. *Problemas pastorales en Corinto*. San José, Costa Rica: DEI/SBL, 1996

Grassi, Joseph A. *The Hidden Heroes of the Gospels: Female Counterparts of Jesus*. Minneapolis: The Liturgical Press, 1989.

Hebblethwaite, Margaret. *Six New Gospels: New Testament Women Tell Their Stories*. Boston: Cowley Publications, 1994.

*Order from the General Board of Global Ministries Service Center. For complete ordering information, see page 182.

*Hollies, Linda. *Jesus and Those Bodacious Women: Life Lessons from One Sister to Another.* Cleveland: United Church Press, 1998. (#3138, $11.95)

Horsley, Richard A. *Galilee: History, Politics, People.* Valley Forge, Penn.: Trinity Press International, 1995.

Jenkins, Simon. *Nelson's 3-D Bible Mapbook.* Nashville: Thomas Nelson Publishers, 1995.

*Killen, Patricia O'Connell. *Finding Our Voices: Women, Wisdom, and Faith.* New York: The Crossroad Publishing Co., 1997. (#3119, $15.95)

*Leonard, Ann. *Seeds 2: Supporting Women's Work Around the World.* New York: The Feminist Press, 1995. (#3163, $12.95)

Malina, Bruce and Richard L. Rohrbaugh. *Social Science Commentary on the Synoptic Gospels.* Minneapolis: Fortress Press, 1992.

Moltmann-Wandel, Elisabeth. *The Women Around Jesus.* New York: The Crossroad Publishing Co., 1982.

Newsom, Carol A. and Sharon H. Ringe, eds. *The Women's Bible Commentary.* Louisville: Westminster John Knox Press, 1992.

Osiek, Carolyn and David L. Balch. *Families in the New Testament World.* Louisville: Westminster John Knox Press, 1997.

Ricci, Carla. *Mary Magdalene and Many Others: Women Who Followed Jesus.* Minneapolis: Fortress Press, 1994.

Ricciuti, Gail Anderson and Rosemary Catalano Mitchell. *Birthings and Blessings II: More Liberating Worship Services for the Inclusive Church.* New York: The Crossroad Publishing Co., 1993.

Richter Reimer, Ivoni. *Vida de Mulheres na Sociedade e na Igreja.* São Paulo, Brazil: Paulinas, 1995.

Ringe, Sharon. *Luke*. Louisville: Westminster John Knox Press, 1995.

Ruether, Rosemary Radford. *Introducing Redemption in Christian Feminism*. Cleveland: The Pilgrim Press, 2000.

Schottroff, Luise. *Lydia's Impatient Sisters: A Feminist Social History of Early Christianity*. Louisville: Westminster John Knox Press, 1995.

_____. *Mulheres no Novo Testamento. Exegese numa Perspectiva Feminista*. São Paulo, Brazil: Paulinas, 1995.

Schüssler Fiorenza, Elisabeth. *In Memory of Her: A Feminist Theological Reconstruction of Christian Origins*. New York: The Crossroad Publishing Co., 1994.

Tunc, Suzanne. *También las mujeres seguían a Jesús*. Santander, Spain: Sal Terrae, 1999.

Watson, Elizabeth G. *Wisdom's Daughters: Stories of Women Around Jesus*. Cleveland: The Pilgrim Press, 1997.

*Wilson, Lois Miriam. *Stories Seldom Told*. Northstone Publishing, Inc., 1997. (#3090, $14.95)

Winter, Miriam Therese. *The Gospel According to Mary*. New York: The Crossroad Publishing Co., 1993.

_____, *WomanPrayer/WomanSong*. Oak Park, Ill.: Meyer-Stone Books, 1987.

_____, *WomanWord: A Feminist Lectionary and Psalter, Women of the New Testament*. New York: The Crossroad Publishing Co., 1991.

Winter, Miriam Therese, Adair Lummis and Allison Stokes. *Defecting in Place: Women Claiming Responsibility for Their Own Spiritual Lives*. New York: The Crossroad Publishing Co., 1994.

Yamasaki, April. *Remember Lot's Wife and Other Unnamed Women of the Bible*. Elgin, Ill.: Brethren Press, 1991.

United Methodist and UMW Resources

The Book of Resolutions of the United Methodist Church, 2000 (Cokesbury at 1-800-672-1789, $14.00)

COSROW: visit the United Methodist General Commission on Status and Role of Women web site for resources related to topics in this study: **http://umc.org/gcsrw**

*Dougherty, Mary Agnes. *My Calling To Fulfill: Deaconesses in the United Methodist Tradition*. New York: General Board of Global Ministries, The United Methodist Church, 1997. (#2656, $9.95)

New World Outlook, the mission magazine of The United Methodist Church, $15.00 a year (six issues); $26.00 for two years. See *Response* for combination subscription information.

Response, the magazine for United Methodist Women. Subscriptions, $12.00 a year (11 issues); $22.00 for two years. In combination with *New World Outlook*, $25.00 a year; $45.00 special two-year rate. Also, a 30th Anniversary CD-ROM is available (see below).

They Went Out Not Knowing: 100 Women in Mission. New York: General Board of Global Ministries, The United Methodist Church, 1986. (#3806, $3.25)

*CD-ROM: *Ten Best Books on the History of United Methodist Women* (#2829, $40.00). Includes *They Went Out Not Knowing and My Calling To Fulfill*, along with 8 others.

*CD-ROM: *Response* 30th Anniversary. 330 issues of *Response*, The Voice of Women in Mission (January 1969-December 1998) (#2821; $15 subscriber, $30 non-subscriber).

United Methodist General Commission on Archives and History. Visit the web site, particularly for women's ordination under "Resources": **http://gcah.org**

Video–*Theressa Hoover: Through the Test of Time*. A vivid histroy of women in mission. Order from the Office of Electronic Media, Room 1331, 475 Riverside Drive, NY, NY. 1-212-870-3781.

*Video–*Theressa Hoover: A Woman with PURPOSE* (#3004, $15.00). A current interview with this pioneering former head of the Women's Division.

Online Resources

*(Note: Many Web sites are frequently updated. Sometimes the site names or other details change. The information offered here is accurate as of April 2001. The Women's Division will keep an up-to-date list of links on its Web site at: **http://gbgm.umc.org/umw/jesus andwomen**. If you encounter problems, use the e-mail address there to communicate with staff.)*

For the Women's Division Web page on the spiritual growth study on Corinthians (2001), see: **http://gbgm-umc.org/umw/corinthians/** This page contains information on the social and political context of early church women, and links to other sites. You can also click on several maps here.

(Also check the lists of Online Resources in the 2001 study book *Conflict and Community in the Corinthian Church* [#2869, $4.50] for more sites on church communities in the New Testament period; see pages 71 and 120.)

For Mark Goodacre's excellent, comprehensive New Testament Gateway site: **www.ntgateway.com/women/index.htm** (This page also has links under Women and Gender to many of the others listed here.)

The excellent site *Diotima: Materials for Study on Women and*

Gender in the Ancient World has a good section on Biblical Studies. Also includes a section on Images for great painting, sculpture and architecture. It now resides at **Stoa.org** – see: **http://www.stoa.org/diotoma**

For excellent resources on Ancient or Women's history, look at Paul Halsell's site on the Fordham University server and click on Ancient or Women: **http://www.fordham.edu/halsell**

The PBS Frontline program "From Jesus to Christ" has several useful pages, including reflections by Elaine Pagels and Elizabeth Clark: *The First Christians: Roles for Women:* **http://www.pbs.org/wgbh/pages/frontline/shows/religion/first/roles.html**
Another page is *Women in Ancient Christianity: The New Discoveries* written by Karen King. Others provide useful maps or timelines: see **~religion/maps/**

For a great page on *Palestine in the Time of Jesus: Social Structures and Social Conflicts* by K.C. Hanson and Douglas E. Oakman (based on their book of the same title), see: **http://www.stolaf.edu/people/kchanson/ptj.html**

For summaries of books on women's issues, see the Sunshine for Women site: **http://www.pinn.net/sunshine/book-sum/booksum.html**

A new scholarly page called *Lectio Difficilior: The European Electric Journal for Feminist Exegesis* is available in English as well as French and German from the University of Berne in Switzerland. Some interesting articles are introduced by a paragraph in German but the text is in English.
See: **http://www.lectio.unibe.ch/**
Click on Archives to see lists of articles; the journal is published twice a year.

For a comprehensive art gallery of paintings through the ages, see CGFA at **http://sunsite.dk/cgfa//**
Click on painting title or artist's name.

For a bibliography called *IOUDAIOS-L*, Introductory Readings for the Study of Judaism in the Greco-Roman Period (which includes Early Christian and Gnostic Literature), compiled by faculty at Bar-Ilan University in Israel, see: **http://faculty.biu.ac.il/**

The Authors

Elsa Tamez is presently professor of biblical studies at the Latin American Biblical University in San José, Costa Rica, and a member of the research team at DEI (Ecumenical Research Department). A native of Mexico, she has been living in Costa Rica for over 25 years. She is a Methodist.

Elsa is known for her contribution to the field of contextual biblical hermeneutics and participates in Bible study workshops in various Latin American countries. She was a member of the Commission on Ecumenical Theological Education of the World Council of Churches for 14 years, and is a member of the Association of Third World Theologians.

Elsa has written numerous books and articles that have been translated into various languages. Among her books that have been translated into English are *Bible of the Oppressed* (1982); *The Scandalous Message of James* (1989); *The Amnesty of Grace* (1993); and *When the Horizons Close: Rereading Ecclesiastes* (2000).

In 1990 Elsa received her Doctoral Degree in Theology from the University of Lausanne, Switzerland. She received a Licentiate in Theology from the Latin American Biblical Seminary in 1979. In 1986, she received a Licentiate in Literature and Linguistics from the National University of Costa Rica. Elsa is married and has two children. She resides in San José, Costa Rica.

Sallie M. Cuffee teaches in the Doctor of Ministry and Master of Divinity program at New York Theological Seminary. In May of 2000, she completed her Ph.D. at Union Theological Seminary in New York City in the area of Christian Ethics. Her dissertation research focused upon the feminist subject "Redemption of Justice in Women's Experience." Sallie received her Master of Divinity degree from Wesley Theological Seminary in Washington, D.C. While at Union, much of her academic studies contributed to her practical involvement in the broad areas of human rights, women's rights, environmental issues, and racial justice. Her commitment to social justice has been recognized with a number of awards, among them the Martin Luther King, Jr. Award. Presently, Sallie works with several religious non-governmental organizations (NGOs) in New York City to facilitate their visible, concrete participation in the United Nations' World Conference on Racism in Durham, South Africa, 2001.

A Women's Division publication produced by the
General Board of Global Ministries, The United Methodist Church

Please mail order with check payable to:
SERVICE CENTER
PO BOX 691328
CINCINNATI OH 45269-1328

COSTS FOR SHIPPING AND HANDLING:
Sale items, total order:

$25 or less, add $4.00
$25.01-$60, add $5.00
$60.01-$100, add $6.00
Over $100, add 6%

Free items:
50 copies or less, $3.00
51-400, $4.00
Over 400, $1.00 per 100
Revised formula effective May 15, 2001

For billed or credit card orders:
Call toll free: 1-800-305-9857
If billing is requested, a $1.50 billing fee will be added.
Fax orders: 1-513-761-3722

**SERVICE CENTER
7820 READING ROAD CALLER NO 1800
CINCINNATI OH 45222-1800**

Processed Chlorine free paper

$4.50   AC/LE 5/01   Stock #2964